SOUTHERNERS
Do Not Row

A Boomer's Fitness Tale

SCOTT COLLINS

Introduction

In Scott's book, I could not help but remember my first years of rowing. I cracked up multiple times as I drew parallels between our rowing experiences. This book is a necessary read for beginners and seasoned rowers. Scott's book puts into perspective how different the world of rowing is when first entered, and how good it feels when you see reason to stay in it.

Here are some of my own experiences that came to me when I discovered Scott's rowing journey. My first day of rowing occurred in the middle of winter in Fontainebleau, France. I was 13 years old. Rarely was there snow where I lived, but the morning of my first rowing stroke there was... Snow and learning how to row at the same time did not make sense to me. Who wants to get wet when the temperatures are low enough to be in a snowball fight? That morning three masters in the age range of 30 to 50 took me under their wing and placed me in a coxed river 4 called a "Yolette". They loved how big I was and how large my hands were. I didn't need oars, my hands were big enough, they joked. I took off my sneakers and was told to strap into the shoes attached to the boat. What an odd idea to be tied down like that. I felt trapped, what if the boat were to flip, what a horrible thought, and all that in winter. If we were to sink wouldn't we immediately die of hypothermia? I held onto the sweep oar with a death grip, somehow it felt like my safety blanket. I survived.

Southerners Do Not Row

Not long after my first row I was initiated to the single scull, "le skiff" as it is called in French. I still remember my first time as if it were yesterday. That day I noticed how strong the spring current in the Seine was and it did not make me any more confident. What if I capsized and a large river monster lurked under the murky water and had me for lunch. My confidence was rattled further when I saw the narrow skiff I was about to use to gain my single sculling stripes. How do I fit "in" that boat when my rear was wider than the hull. I was explained that one sits "on" the boat. That made no sense to me either, doesn't that make the whole deal top heavy, unstable and easier to flip? "Ne t'inquiete pas, Xeno"- don't worry, I was told. The sculls which looked like oversized tooth picks would help me with stability, yeah right. I hoped that I would get two wooden sweep oars, which are heavier and could certainly float me in case I flipped and had to fight for my life. Sitting for the first time in a single scull felt insecure and uncomfortable which gave me the same sensation as my fear of heights- nausea. I survived.

After several winter and wet spring rows came the first warm day. I showed up with tennis shorts that sported two large pockets to put balls into. That turned out to be a big mistake. Every stroke got caught in those darn pockets. That evening my mom came to the rescue and sewed the pockets shut. Soon after that I got my first spandex rowing shorts a staple item for water rowers. Rowing fashion was a non-issue until five years, and three world championship later. When I become a freshman at Brown University, most of my Swiss national team training cloths were bright red and white. My spandex leggings were bright blue. These colors made me stand out like a sore thumb and my fellow oarsman joked that I, the "fuzzy foreigner", looked like Captain America. I survived.

Like Scott, I was lactate tested too. I particularly enjoyed his take on the lactate test results. I remember, when I was 17 years old and underwent my first such test. It was odd to voluntarily "give blood" (although it is a tiny amount) to someone other than a doctor or a nurse. After testing, I asked how I stacked up to the international elite, and got a bitter sweet answer. It was explained to me that I had great potential but that it would take several years before I would match the world's best. As a teenager, several years seemed like a lifetime. I wanted to be a rowing machine before I turned 18... I stuck to the training and followed my heart rate monitor religiously. I did more than just survive.

Rowing would not be complete without coaches. Coaches I had a few and here is what I remember so of them saying.

Michel Colard from the Association Fontainebleau Avon said to make us remember that we had legs to use when rowing: "Allez pousse sur les gibolles," which meant in colloquial French, "come on, push on your legs."

Harry Mahon, national team coach for Switzerland and New Zealand, was instrumental in teaching me how to stay relaxed during all-out effort, "Xeno, hang of the leg drive, relax the face, catch now, etc."

Scott Roop from Brown University motivated us for racing by saying, "Smile when you get half way into the race, they are hurting, and you move on."

Steve Gladstone from Brown University with his deep radio voice, "guys, become complete watermen."

Marty Aitken, my coach for the Olympics in which I won gold and silver, "Xeno, keep the contrast between leg drive and recovery, catch where you reach to, do your miles and bank them, cop you later, hit them hard when it hurts them the most."

I was also coached by: David Martin from U.K., Jean Pierre Leroux & Pierre Fenie from France, Martin Dummermuth, Eugen Schmidt and Felix Boller from Switzerland. After reading the list of names I need to confess that some were much better coaches than others. But as an athlete I always looked at the glass half full. I lived by the motto, what does not kill me makes me stronger.

In 1996, I won Olympic gold in the men's single scull. By then, I had heard how to row in five different languages. I had ten different coaches. My life time mileage was roughly 31,000 kilometers, 19,000 miles, a little more than six times from New York City, to Los Angeles. I am still alive and kicking... I mean rowing.

Today, I introduce newbies to the sport of rowing on a weekly basis. I pride myself in creating a non-intimidating environment by using positive verbalization on how to apply power efficiently by using safe technique. It is extremely rewarding to witness changes in people who adopt rowing as a lifestyle. Their health, state of mind, and their general quality of life improves dramatically. Rowing and its seated nature welcomes people of all ages and fitness levels. It is one of those rare sports that delivers real positive results and is immune to age and ability discrimination.

Thank you, Scott, for sharing your story.

Xeno Muller
Olympic Gold and Silver Medalist
Men's Single Scull

Contents

1

Twisted Steel and Sex Appeal?

In July 2007, I finally gave into Meredith, my wife, and went to the doctor for a check up. I had been having chest pains that I attributed to my blame-thrower boss. Meredith had been encouraging me for months to get to a cardiologist. Mom, a retired MD, was following my wife's lead and had started to put the pressure on as well. Mom can be particularly brutal in her health assessments with details of all the things that could possibly be wrong. Plaque in arteries, congenital problems, asthma-related issues, and my eating habits were all on her hit list. Despite these concerns and my chest pain, I was sure I was a healthy specimen. Undoubtedly, the doctor would believe me when he saw the rippling hulk that lurked beneath my tee shirt—twisted steel and sex appeal.

Others who knew me thought I was a bit overweight; I was an asthmatic, ex-smoker who normally worked sixty to seventy-five hours a week. I lifted weights a couple of times a week, played golf, and walked a fair amount around the city of New York to get from one spot to another. But I was the only one who thought this resembled any sort of fitness routine.

In order to stop Meredith from worrying, I made the appointment for a check up. I took off work, drove to New Haven to see a Yale cardiologist whom my wife and her gynecologist had conspired to find for me. As I drove to the appointment, I imagined that twenty minutes into the exam the doctor and I would be laughing heartily. After the exam we would conclude that it was only stress causing my symptoms, and he would give me a prescription to body slam my overly coifed boss and his lollipop guild confederates.

We started with history and proceeded into the exam. This will be over soon, I laughingly thought to myself. About ten minutes later he gave his verdict. Smiles were dancing in my head. No need to worry he would say. You are a perfect example of how we want folks in their fifties to live.

Unfortunately, he began to talk seriously. While he was pretty sure that my chest pains were stress-related, there were some underlying problems. Uh oh. He said I had to lose some weight. I guess the twisted steel looked more like middle-age bloat. My blood pressure and heart rate were both bordering on the danger zone. I needed to change my lifestyle and eating habits. The good doctor starting firing questions on the amount of cardio exercise I was getting and what I was eating. He turned me over to a nurse who started in on the same line of questioning. Please detail your daily eating habits for me. Let's talk about your exercise regimen—daily, weekly, monthly. When was the last time you had a pulmonary workup for your asthma? We are going to schedule a stress test so we can rule out any underlying problems.

My self-image was taking serious whacking here. Surely this was what an overcautious doctor did with every fifty-three year old. As the son of two MDs, I had lived my whole life with hospitals, doctors, and diagnoses. I was convinced that I was getting the standard stuff to justify the years the doctor had spent in school, residency, and organic chemistry classes while the rest of us lived, loved, went on road trips, and took the easiest college courses that would lead to a degree and a job.

I left the doctor with a stack of paper—diet suggestions, exercise regimens, appointments for blood and stress tests. I got into my car and drove home. It was three in the afternoon when I got home. Meredith was there when I came upstairs from the garage. On seeing the stack of stuff in my hands, I got the look. You know the one—that says that judging by the stack of paper (which I should have tossed out the car window), there was a problem. That she was right. And now she could feel lovingly superior in her judgment while mothering me to make me feel better. This was going to be the marital equivalent of dentistry without Novocain.

I started slowly explaining what the doctor had said and the nurse's suggestions. Meredith was kind and non-judgmental—so far. We discussed the next steps. I listened. We talked. I nodded. I joked. But I was not a believer. It was clear to everyone but me that I was going to have to begin an all-out exercise regimen. But I had not accepted cardio fitness into my life yet. In a couple of weeks all this worry, all this angst, all these blood pressure readings would be forgotten. Once we do the stress test and they see what an incredible specimen I am, this will all be over. Only one more week to go and everything will be normal. Even that short, over styled boss of mine was looking better to me. Honey, pour me a Jack Daniels while I see if we have any steaks in the freezer.

2

Round 2

A week had passed, and it was time for the stress test. To pacify the situation at home Meredith and I talked about exercises I should be doing. No, I was told, golf was not an option. No, I said, I do not like running that much. What about a bike? Oh yeah, cold weather. But what about a stationary bike? Nah. Those seats are prostate bangers. Well, the wife said, let's see what the stress test says, but you have to make a decision.

So off I went, hopeful that the test would quell the storm of cardio fitness that was tossing my ship of state.

Sadly it did not, and I dejectedly crept home. I knew I was going to have to deal with this siren song—time to get fit, you can not delay, you are at that age. The "at that age" thing hurt. Come on. I am not that old. It is not like I am over the hill. I am virile—a bull of a man. I bet I could still run a 4.6" forty-yard dash. After all, the older I get, the faster I was. This is crazy.

I knew that dealing with the better half on getting back in shape was going to be tough. She was still within breathing distance of her weight in her early twenties. She could still peel off an eight-minute mile like nothing. She had taken up rowing a few years ago and had turned herself into a competitive athlete. She was winning a few races and finishing well in the bigger races, despite being early in her rowing career. She had already tapped me for a German single shell (a boat that one person rows) so she could get even better. In other words, she is sort of a sports force of nature, and I knew I was in trouble.

It is not that I have anything against getting in shape. It was just that I never liked sports that require large amounts of cardio work. Run a mile? Okay, but no further. Better to play a sport where the plays, points, or otherwise do not last too long. I had that notion from youth that says that real athletes do not do cardio-based sports. Real athletes do ball sports. Only those who cannot throw, catch, bat, run or shoot do cardio sports. And I had another excuse—I was an asthmatic. I can't do that cardio crud; I will wheeze and be sucking on my nebulizer for an hour.

But now my force-of-nature wife was bolstered by scientific reinforcement that was blowing an evil wind my way. I was going to have to take up a sport. Why not rowing? It's on the water; I like to fish and swim. You sit on your can, so it can't be too stressful to the body. You are not going to fall on the pavement and get all skinned up or die at the hands of some rabid, late-to-work driver who thinks you are taking up too much road. You can row on machines in the winter in front of the TV; therefore, football and other important televised events can still be consumed. This is what I was saying out loud to the force-of-nature mate of mine.

But deep down inside I was thinking other thoughts. I grew up in the South. We do not row. Only elitist Northeasterners do that. Southerners race boats or cars, shoot birds and deer, and yell like crazy people at all sporting events. And while all this is going on, we are consuming vast quantities of fried food and drinking stately quantities of alcohol. We do not sit backward on our bohunkus and slap hatchets with long handles into the water trying to propel a boat with nothing but our own muscles.

Slowly, an evil plan helped relieve my cognitive dissonance. I would tell Meredith that I would take up rowing. I would make a valiant attempt to be a part of this community of health freaks. But time was on my side. Eventually, she would get sick of seeing me at the rowing club, flailing away vainly while in my most authoritarian way telling her what she was doing wrong with her rowing stroke. She would be embarrassed that my athletic ability would soar to heights with which she was not familiar. She wouldn't like the fact that the whole club would be focusing their attention on me and my prowess. She would surely get sick of suggestions that we row together. Constantly hearing "Scott is doing really well" would grate on her psychology so much that I could slowly give up the sport without any worries about my health and well being. She would just be happy to have me gone.

Finally, I hatched a plan that I was sure could be put into effect with a reasonable amount of low effort and whose success was guaranteed. I could row, succeed modestly due to my incredible athletic talent, subtly turn Meredith off to the idea of mate rowing, and slink away to pursue more enjoyable ventures. Perfect.

3

Rub a Dub Tub

Having hatched a perfect plan, I began to work with Meredith to create the solution for my rowing problem. I needed to learn this sport in order to perform it. For the uninitiated, let me give you some background on the wonders of rowing. My initial impression was that you get into a boat and start to whack away. Nothing hard about that. I figured I would get more efficient with the oars over time, and it would be off to stardom in my chosen sport.

Unfortunately it's not that simple. First, the physics of the sport are somewhat challenging. A racing single, built for one rower, is about twelve inches wide, twenty-seven feet long, and weighs about thirty pounds. Oars (called sculls when you use two of them or sweeps when you use one) are about ten feet long. The oars propel you and help balance the boat. But put an oar in the water wrong, lean the wrong way, or make any number of other mistakes and you can wind up in a flip, which leaves you wet and embarrassed. Also you are secured to the boat by a pair of shoes that are screwed to something called a foot stretcher and are velcroed tight to your feet. As a rower becomes better, there is less worry about the shoe issue. But as a beginner, it feels like being glued to the wing of a plane that was sure to crash.

So why not start out in a bigger boat, one for four or eight rowers. These boats are wider, heavier, and more stable. So let's start here. But experienced rowers hate rowing with inexperienced ones. Beginner rowers get everyone wet with their lack of quality blade work. Beginners do not have much power or stamina, so all the other rowers suffer as a result. Beginning rowers have no balance. The boat, therefore, rocks and rolls all over, making it hard for the more experienced to even get their oars into the water in a normal way. So unless you have a large group of beginners to jam into a boat together, most other rowers will run from a beginner.

So I began like most beginners over the age of thirty—in a shorter, wider single-rower boat. These boats allow you to work on the mechanics of the stroke from a more stable platform. But there is a downside. The boats are called tubs by better rowers who immediately identify you as a beginner. Since 99 percent of all rowers do not want to row with a beginner, rowing this tub is like a having a huge zit in the middle of your forehead before the prom. There is nothing more satisfying than getting out of this tub.

As I slowly learned all the zit on the forehead issues from my wife, I realized that there were not many options but to bite the bullet and row a tub like a fifty-three-year-old beginner. It was not that exciting, but to perfect my plan to slink away from this sport I had to learn to row effectively.

Meredith suggested that we take a long weekend at a rowing camp, where I could learn to row out of the bright light of day that would surround the learning process at her rowing club. Yes, I thought. I will spend three or four days working on the perfect stroke. At the end of this session I'll be almost qualified to row with my new former Olympic rowing friends. We will joke about the small number of days it took for me to be famous. Veni,vidi,vici as Caesar would say. They'll be amazed at how quickly I learned, but I will shyly admit that others have done it faster. You do not want people to think you have a big ego about your immense talent, after all.

So off we went to Craftsbury, a rowing camp in northern Vermont. One of the things that surprised me about rowing was the amount of resources that are committed to this sport for the older rower. Were there other camps like this? Do a lot of new people come into this sport? Do people other than beginners come to these camps? Yes, Yes and Yes…. my wife informed me. So we packed and drove about four hours to northern Vermont over the Labor Day weekend.

We arrived early Thursday afternoon, checked in, and went to our cabin. Everything there was Vermont chic, which is to say that it is not chic at all. A clean, Spartan cabin with one bathroom that was about as fancy as my first apartment's bath. I could already feel the need for a beer welling up in my throat when Meredith told me that we had a meeting that afternoon, and we would do one class on the water. Joy. I changed into shorts and a tee shirt and proceeded to the dock.

On the dock I was met with my first sucker punch. I guess in agreeing to row, I never really focused on the attire common to rowing. My baggy shorts and loose fitting tee shirt were not going to be acceptable after this weekend. Rowers wear tight, mid-thigh spandex shorts combined with tighter fitting tops typically fortified with a heavy dose of polyester and spandex. While there is an explanation for this (so the shorts will not get caught in the seat tracks while the seat rolls back and forth and so your hands or thumbs will not get hooked on your loose non slippery shirt as you pull the oars into your body), I really did not care at that specific moment. All I could think about was what an idiot I was. I never bothered to ask Meredith about the clothes she wore for rowing. She looked great in all this tight stuff, but I did not even think it was common to other rowers. How am I going to get my large American ass into those shorts? I looked at all those skinny rowers, and then there was me—a bloated, alcohol basted fifty-ish Southerner whose six pack came in a bag.

As I digested the fashion pain I was experiencing, the coaches talked about the weekend. We were going to have a number of classes on the water: three a day on Friday and Saturday, and one on Sunday. We would also be having video reviews of our rowing and classes on nutrition, stretching and yoga. Great! Not only is the whole Craftsbury world going to know that I carry a Firestone with me at all times, they are going to quickly figure out that my hands and toes were strangers. This whole rowing thing was slowly beginning to feel less like a sport and more like a lifestyle. A crunchy, happy, wholesome lifestyle full of a bunch of hippies who do not believe in eating healthy quantities of dead animal flesh. They really enjoy their yoga and stretching—not football, baseball, or cage fighting. I began to wonder when I could get to a TV and watch an SEC football game. Oh, yeah-there was no TV in the cabin.

What am I doing here?????? I still had faith in the plan, the one that allowed me to quit with respect. But the foundation was beginning to feel like it was built on sand.

We went to the dock and the coaches divided the rowers into groups. I went into the newbie group. Thankfully, I was not the only one. I could share my pain with others. My coach assigned me a boat and oars that were identified by a number so that it would be easy for me to find them again. I also learned that our first task was to take a swim test. But not just any swim test. We had to get in one of the tubs, push a few feet off the dock, flip it, and try to get back in. I knew that I would be okay until the reentry of the boat. Casually, I didn't volunteer for the test until I had seen enough of the others struggle to get back into the boat. I figured that visual learning of the right and wrong ways to do this would allow me not to make too big of a mess of my reentry.

After watching ten newbies get back into the boat with various degrees of success, it was my turn. I got in, pushed away, and flipped the boat. I was not prepared for how easy it was to tip the boat. A lean of the shoulder and small slide of the seat, and I was in the cold Vermont water. And this was the tub—the boat that was the equivalent of training wheels. It was way too easy to flip. From the water I grabbed the oars in one hand. Put my hands on the gunnel as instructed and kicked up my body to lay over the boat sideways. I was somehow supposed to squirrel my legs into the boat with care not to put too much weight into the bottom of the boat. Too much weight in the bottom can cause the boat to crack and sink. I kicked, tried to roll my butt into the seat, and ended back in the water on the other side. A truly athletic move. I couple of more tries yielded similar results. A sigh from the coach was the sign that I had worn out his patience, but I had let him know that I could swim well enough to wrestle this fiberglass and carbon fiber beast of a boat all day.

Our next mission, which I gladly accepted, was to get our boats and oars from their respective racks and bring them down to the docks. I had watched Meredith carry her boat by herself. If she can do it... I went to the rack and tried to get the tub on my shoulder as she had done with her racing single. Little did I know that dealing with the tub was a lot harder. The coach came over to give me hand, knowing instinctively that I was about to get in trouble. I guess I was sending out the "this guy is too stupid to know what to do" pheromone. We took the boat down to the water. He asked me where my oars were. I said there are still in the boathouse. I got the smile. The one that says I am really clueless. I soon learned that you bring your oars down first. Otherwise, the boat will float off the dock if you leave the boat to get your oars. Oh! I was shown how to put the oars in the oarlocks and some other basics. I got gingerly into the boat and pushed off the dock with a great deal of anticipation. I felt that at any moment I would be up to my nose in cool, clear Vermont H_2O. Somehow I took a stroke, feathered the blade so that the flat side was pointing to the sky when the oars came out of the water, pulled myself up the slide, and put my oars back into the water for another stroke. Yesssss. My plan was coming together. This weekend was genius. I would soon be rowing with the best.

Another few strokes and I hit a really ugly one. Complete disaster. Only by the grace of God had I remained dry. One Hail Mary and I started again. Another few strokes and I heard someone yelling my name. What? Watch where I am going? Note to Scott—I am facing the rear. I have to figure out a way to row and look over my shoulder to understand which oar I need to put pressure on to steer. Now this is interesting. Okay, I got it. Look at me. I am rowing. I bet I am flying compared to others. It has taken me about five minutes to go about one hundred yards. That is pretty good. A little more efficiency and I am on my way.

At that point I saw Meredith. She put the oars in one hand and waved. I did the same but with not quite the same ease or form. She rowed over and asked how it was going. I spoke confidently. She knew better. Off she went. Enjoy yourself now, I thought, because soon there will be a new sheriff in town.

I rowed and rowed. I saw people pass me going one way, and then I would see them passing me going the other way. If people were passing me going both ways, there had to be an end to this lake. But before I got there, one of the coaches pulled along side in a chase boat. The wake of the boat could not have been more that six inches tall, but it was enough to almost flip me. And then the son of a gun wanted to talk about things I needed to do to improve my stroke. Didn't he realize I was hanging on for dear life? Come on.

The coach instructed "Do not stop at the finish." The finish is not really a finish. It is just called that. As soon as your oars come out of the water at the finish, feather them and immediately start you way back up the slide. Do not pause there, and do not forget to start the move up the slide with your body. Get your body in a forward lean before you break your knees. Got it? Okay. Try that for a few strokes and then we will film you.

I could hear my son texting my brain—OMG. Do what again? No! Put that damn camera down. I am in trouble. At least smile. Wow, am I ever sweating. Whew, he drove away.

For the rest of the row that day I worked on the coaching points. Or at least my version of the instruction. I got to the end of the lake and back. I was probably one of the last three off the lake. I went through the embarrassment of docking really badly and almost flipping. I put my boat and oars away. I thanked the coach and went back to my cabin. But Meredith was not there. I had forgotten the stretching class. So I did my version of a jog back to the boathouse to get the full immersion rowing experience.

The coach had already begun the stretching session by the time I arrived. I fell in the back and started. While I would not describe myself as a rubber band, I was surprised that there was not a huge difference between myself and some of the other men. Maybe I am more flexible than I thought. Nah. I must be with a bunch inflexible guys like myself. In any event it was not that embarrassing, and I survived. I also had to admit that the stretching sure helped everything feel better. Who would have thought that the mere act of rowing oneself back and forth on a lake could be that stressful? But I was tired, and I could tell that I would be stiff and sore tomorrow.

Back to the cabin for a shower. When I got there I quickly asked my wife how many times she had been around the lake. Three times? Wow. It took a while to sink in. So she was more than three times faster than me. She went on the water before me and came off way before I did. I suck.

After a shower and a painful dressing due to my sore muscles, we went to dinner. All the Craftsbury campers eat in a central dining hall. Hearty wholesome Yankee food—nothing fried, no big slabs of beef barbequed to a charcoal richness. We had lots of pasta, a vegetarian alternative, some chicken, whole grain this and that, salads, and vegetables. Well, at least I ought to lose some weight. Dinner was a fairly painless affair. Nice conversation with a bunch of nice people. It struck me, though, that for most of the folks there, rowing was as much about a healthy lifestyle as it was a sport. Most of the folks were non-collegiate rowers who had taken up the sport later in life as a way to be fit. Most had gotten sucked into the sport and were committed to racing, rowing better, and being fit. Most trained year round, monitored their performance, and strove to succeed. Not everyone was a superstar, but they made an effort and tried to improve. I can respect that. But as I thought about it, I wondered who else would be at this camp but the committed.

We returned to our cabin after dinner. I read about the program describing the next day. I read a little of a book I had brought. At about eight thirty, I turned over to turn out the light. Meredith and I were both dozing off while reading, and I was wiping drool from the side of my mouth.

Morning came quickly. After a quick snack, we were on the water again by seven thirty. More work. Although this day was better than the day before, I still was at the back of the pack. Sweat was pouring off of me. I was a slow rower, and working harder was not resulting in much progress on the water. I certainly was not piling up the meters on the water. I was being passed constantly by 110-pound kids and middle-aged women and seventy-year-old men. Unlike other sports I had played, trying harder did little to improve the situation. The harder I worked, the faster my stroke fell apart and put me in jeopardy of flipping. Soon a coach came by in a launch. A few suggestions, and he was on his way to the next rower. Hey dude! Stay with me. I have to get better if I am going to put the plan into effect.

I kept whacking away at the oars. Splashing myself and the bow of the boat. I had done one lap around the lake and was halfway into the second when someone in a launch came to get me off the water. As I looked around, I realized that I was again close to the last one on the water. On top of that I realized I probably went a shorter distance than all but a few. Add to that, I was hurting. How could a sport where all you do is pull on a couple of oars cause any kind of pain? My hands were blistering.

My back and shoulders were feeling the strain. I was working hard but not moving the boat very well.

Time for breakfast. Do not forget to stretch. Yep that feels better. Honey, does it get any better than this? Meredith consoled me and offered some advice on the blisters, but I had the feeling she was holding back some vital counsel. Is there some rower's code that you have to get through a certain amount of pain before the more experienced will impart their golden wisdom on you? How does a sport that has no contact cause this much pain? What was she not telling me?

We went to another hearty, wholesome meal. Was I the only one seriously in need of some salty cured meat and a heavy dose of butter? They call this breakfast? Fruit, whole grains, eggs. Lots of talk surrounded our table about plans for the upcoming winter training. I sat and listened. What is a rowing training plan? Everyone was talking about their favorite regatta in the fall head race season. Regattas are races in which rowers from around the country compete. Some liked the Schuylkill, some the Head of the Chattahoochee, some liked the Head of the Housatonic. Everyone liked the Head of the Charles and hoped they got in this year. This was all new to me. I knew Meredith went to regattas but never paid to much attention to all the goings on.

I asked what the head part of the regatta means. Does it refer to a part of the river? I guess I had just committed a rowing sin. Most looked at me as if I had just parachuted from a different planet. Meredith kindly stepped in and explained that this was my first weekend rowing. I learned that a head race was longer than a sprint race. They were typically 4000 to 5000 meters, while a sprint race was 1000 meters for the masters division. The head races dominate the fall season, when it is a bit cooler for the approximately twenty minutes of hard rowing.

Twenty minutes of hard racing! Really? That is some serious aerobic fitness. I realized that even thinking about doing this was premature. I needed to focus on learning the sport, getting out of that embarrassing tub. I needed to figure out how to get my oars in and out of the water without splashing the hell out of myself. In my head I was beginning to think of this sport much like I thought about golf. How do you create a fluid stroke that has correct physics? But unlike golf, you have to do this while working physically hard, sweating and breathing like you are about to kick the bucket.

We did the same thing for the rest of the weekend. Row, eat, row, eat, row, eat. Most nights were free time except for the occasional film reviews. The film reviews were painful. A number of very good rowers had come to this session. Not that I would know a good rower from a bad one, but Meredith pointed out which rowers had the strong reputations. I sat in the film sessions listening to the coaches' comments to the better rowers. The comments included: sit more upright at the catch; do not crash the catch; get your blades in the water faster; work on your feather technique. All of it went right over my head. What I did notice was that the other rowers hardly looked like they were rowing. It looked effortless. It was opposite of the flog machine I seemed to be producing.

It was my turn for the critique. I looked like a fat troll in the boat. All six feet one inch of me seemed to be slouched. The coaches were kind, knowing that this was my first weekend. Sit up; more compression at the catch; work on your blade depth; more body swing; do not stop at the finish; and do not feather under the water. These were my comments. Or least those were the comments I heard before the brain shut down from overload. How does anybody conquer this sport? I pulled Meredith aside and told her I was going back to cabin to overdose on Advil and go to sleep.

On the way back to the cabin I railed against God, my fat useless can, my blood pressure, and my cardiologist. I had spent a weekend trying to learn a sport for the taller and less corpulent variety. I was not sure that this sport was for me. I was thinking I should have picked running. All you need are shoes. Any idiot can run. As I am a garden variety idiot, I can surely do it. That back injury and the four bulging discs from a few years ago that resulted in a numb left foot was not a problem. I would just drag it along if it became an issue. Or maybe I would just do the elliptical. No pressure. Thirty minutes of circular movements in a gym with head phones a couple of times a week. Cool. No sin in quitting now. The plan was changing. I was on shaky ground.

Life seemed a little better in the morning. But probably because we were packing and going home that day. We did not do the morning session. Both of us wanted to get home. We loaded clothes, boat, oars and my over worn body into and onto the car for the drive back to Connecticut. We talked about the rowing after a while.

I spilled out my frustrations, my small injuries, and my misunderstandings about the sport. My good wife was patient and kind. I guess she had felt the same when she started. But unlike me, she probably had gutted through it without whining. She could basically row circles around me. And I was whining to her? Buck up, fella. Being a beginner is not fun. Get through the process. How much worse could it be?

Meredith convinced me that the next step was to go back to the rowing club in Norwalk and sign up for some beginner lessons. She told me she had looked into it, and we could do a six-pack of lessons. That would take me into October. By that time I should be able to row with others. Life would be better then.

4

Spandex Graduation

The next weekend Meredith took me to her rowing club and introduced me to the coaches. She did most of the talking as I was not sure what I was asking for exactly. I was told to come the next morning at nine o'clock.

When we got home Meredith showed me the rowing shorts she had bought for me. Spandex laden, tight, mid thigh rowing shorts. Like all men I have no trouble standing in front of a mirror, reminding myself that I look as good as I did at the age of twenty-two. In reality the thought of pulling these over my expanded waistline was less than appealing. Meredith also gave me some really important advice. She begged that I wear some kind of compression short underneath. When I looked at her quizzically, she informed me that women do not really like to see the outline of the men's twig and berries. Really? You can see this. You mean some guys go commando? I figured I had better shut up at this point. I was bordering on asking who and how big. Time to accept my fate.

The next day I puttered around the house as long as possible before heading over to the rowing club. I met my coach. Got my oars and boat, another tub, and went down to the water. I rigged up, pushed off, and almost flipped. All the work I had done the week before had completely seeped from my muscle memory. I somehow got to the center of the river, where the coach in his launch caught up with me. He said start out at half slide. I had no clue what that meant. I sat and looked about as smart as a chimp doing brain surgery for a few seconds. He thankfully picked up that my EEG had flat lined. He stood up, sat backwards in his launch, and did a reasonable impression of half a stroke.

So we started at half a stroke. I had to remember that it was called half slide. I put that in my rowing dictionary. After all, you do not want to sound like the raw rookie meat that you are. He watched me row and after about one hundred yards, he said "three quarters." That did not compute for a second or two. Then the fog in my head cleared and I realized he meant three quarters of a stroke. Oh, yeah. I am rowing now. Right then I stuck an oar or pulled a crab. I have no idea why it is called pulling a crab, or knew what pulling a crab was at that point. Basically, when you oar enters the water at an angle other than ninety degrees, the oar wants to go deep. So when you pull on that crabbed oar, it keeps going deeper and upsets the balance of the boat. I had no clue what to do. I must not be too much of a man, though. No, I did not squeal like a four year old; I basically just stopped. I made no attempt to pull harder, muscle the oar, or any other action that a higher testosterone-laden human would have attempted. I just stopped. And with that stop, the boat sort of righted itself.

Coach raised his eyebrows, smiled and said good job. He then made his hand to look like an oar, put it perpendicular to his other hand, and said, "Like this." Then he put his hand at a non-ninety degree angle and said, "Not like this." I got it. Not a lot of conversation here. Just short and effective instruction. This is good. He let me row, made the necessary corrections, and did not overburden me with all the screw ups he saw. We went to full stroke. We rowed for a bit over an hour, stopping occasional to show me some technical point. Usually the point was demonstrated visually, not verbally. That was okay with me, as I am not sure I could do it without seeing it. In that time on the water I pulled hard, sweat like a pig, and breathed like a marathoner. Yep- this is what cardio is all about. I am sure that my blood pressure has dropped ten points now. When can I go back to my old self? It was only after I came in that I learned from Meredith that I had only rowed about 2000 meters. (Sorry for the meter thing; it is just the way rowers talk.)

Only? That's over a mile. I asked her how far the good rowers went. What? Nine thousand to 10,000 meters! In how long? In the same amount of time? Crap I still suck.

I came back the next weekend. The lessons were similar. Me getting all lathered, hearing and trying to make corrections. Making progress slowly up and down the river. But I was faced on that second day with a unique coaching point. The coach told me to keep my legs together at the catch. This requires some explanation. The catch is the point of the stroke where you are fully compressed (remember the seat slides) with your knees under your chin and a forward lean to your body, trying to get your oars back into the water efficiently. Now the coach was telling me to bring my knees closer together at that point. Well I tried on the next stroke but experienced pain. Man pain. I must have grimaced because the coach started laughing. Now, I am as good a sport as anyone but this was just not that funny. He saw my less-than-pleased look and grabbed himself like a rapper as if to show me where to put things. I got the picture. So not only do I have to wear fruity shorts with some sort of compression wear underneath, now I also have to make an arrangement. What a goofy sport. I again came off the water with the other rowers who had completed a couple of 5k races against my measly 2k effort.

One of the things I learned in these two days is that the experienced rowers tend not to pay you too much attention. None of them want to row with you because you still suck. They see the tub you row and the lights go out. You are basically rookie fodder. One woman would constantly call me "sir" and ask me to help pick this up, move this around, and hold this while she did something else. I felt like her personal boat boy. No introduction. No "thank you for your help." I guess I learned that when an experienced rower older than yourself calls you sir, it is probably some rower code for dope or asshole or some other demeaning name. Finally, Meredith saved me by introducing me to her as her learning-rower husband. While she still asked for help from this rookie, I stopped being her personal slave.

Other folks would give me little more than the time of day. I realize now that it is because so many rookies come and go. It is a bit like being the new private in battle-tested unit. They will talk to you if you survive the blisters, the lessons, the flips, the training and continue to come. This is not to say you get treated badly. It is more like you do not really exist. You are raw, rookie meat.

Five more lessons and three weekends later I was still rowing my 2000 meters on Saturday and Sunday morning. I was still fighting to keep the boat upright. I was still in a tub. I was still the rawest of raw rookies. But I was slowly realizing the pitiful shape I was in. I was working hard to do 2000 meters, while all the non-rookies were putting in 10,000 and looking fresher than myself. Seventy-year-old men and women were passing me as if I was sitting still. I was sure that better rowing skills were necessary, but I was also realizing that I had a fitness issue. Thankfully, at the end of my six-lesson package it was time to get off the water and begin winter training.

5

Double Ugh

At the time I was not real sure what the heck winter training was. I had heard comments about it at Craftsbury, but I still had no real clue. So, as always, I asked rowing wife. Meredith explained that it was the time when we get off the water and work indoors on the ergs (rowing machines), other machines like stationary bike and ellipticals, and do weight training. After my month on the water and about two weeks of the voice in the back of my head telling me I was a pitiful physical specimen, I cannot say that the news was unwelcome. I could come on the weekends to lift weights and ride the recumbent bike and erg. How bad could it be?

Meredith explained, though, that to have an effective winter training session, I would need to get my lactic acid tested.

You can test for this? What does it tell you?

I learned that the point of winter training was to work out in a way that raises the level of work you can do before feeling the negative effects of lactic acid. So what she was proposing was to see a coach who can determine my current level of lactic acid during various workloads. By knowing this I'd be able to work out more effectively over the winter.

Meredith told me she would schedule an appointment on a Saturday or Sunday about two weeks away. In the meantime, she said I should try to get comfortable on the rowing machine so that the machine and I were not strangers. She also suggested that I go online and find resources to create a training plan.

I was not completely unfamiliar with training plans. I had played sports in my youth, and training plans were part of your off-season work. But these plans are just for real athletes. In my mind real athletes played real sports—like football, basketball, wrestling, and other similar sports—the ones you watched on weekend television. Somehow I thought that for rowing, you just rowed a lot and tried to increase your ability to survive the long training sessions. I did not envision that there was much to it.

I was in store for an education.

I went online to look for training plans and was amazed at all the resources. Unfortunately, I understood little of it. The plans talked about training at different heart rates and different rowing times (called splits), like a 2K-race time. There was talk about different intensity levels—something about CAT VI-II or UT2 and LT—or categories called C, R, EXE, INE, and HINE. I was clueless. I bought a heart-rate monitor because at least I understood that different intensities of work caused your heart to beat at different levels. Of course, most humans understand that from the time they are six years old. So this was clearly not a huge intellectual leap.

Not really understanding what to do yet, I would erg for thirty minutes, usually starting on the erg at a 2'30" split and working down to a 2'15" split by the end of the workout. I would be totally whipped after a half hour. I tried to hop on the erg a couple of times during the week after work and a couple of times on the weekend. Twenty to thirty minutes on this contraption seemed like an eternity. And when combined with a little weight lifting and some bike and elliptical work, I was sure that it would be no time to the rowing hall of fame. A couple of months of this and… Well once again, my ego was way ahead of my knowledge base.

In a couple of weeks we took a trip to see Guenter, a former German team rowing coach who is now part of a club near Danbury. Guenter is also the lactic acid test guy. Rower wife explained to me on the way up that we would be erging three or four seven-minute pieces. At the end of each piece, Guenter would prick my ear lobe and measure the lactic acid in my blood. This did not sound too bad, but I was still not sure what the results would yield.

When we got there, Guenter asked that I do a ten-minute warm-up. We would then row three seven minute pieces at increasing intensities. He would start at 110 watts for the first, move to 140 for the second, and end at 160. I had no idea what this watt thing was. Meredith explained that the time splits correspond to a certain wattage. As usual, the explanation was a bit over my head. But I did not want to look too stupid, so I just shut up. As I got on the erg for my ten-minute warm-up, I started to add up the amount of work I would be doing: 10 minutes of warm up + 3x7-minute pieces = 31 minutes. Crap, this is going to be harder that I thought. Thirty minute pieces on the erg were whipping my tail. Time to man up.

We started on the seven-minute pieces after a brief rest following the warm-up. The first was fairly easy. All I had to do was hold the 110 number that showed on the timer screen of the erg. The second was a little more painful. But the final one was work. After each piece I would stop, have my ear pricked and squeezed, rest a couple of minutes and start again. When the last piece was over and the blood had been taken, Guenter handed me a sheet of paper with a graph on it. He told me that my lactate threshold was 155 watts. The paper also had some hieroglyphics on it about heart rates and different intensity levels.

He must have seen the drool rolling off my many chins (or maybe Meredith had told him that I was clueless and to help me) because he started to explain all this to me. He explained the graph first. He said that when rowing over 155 watts, my lactic acid started to build to a level that my body cannot clear it. This was bad because you cannot row above this level for extended periods of time. I was told that the goal of my training is to raise this lactate threshold level. So what I should do is a lot of base training with some threshold work a few times a week. Interesting, but what is base training? As I was thinking about this question, Guenter told me the answer before I asked out loud. He said that about 80 percent of my training should be done in the lower two heart-rate zones he had listed on the sheet, with the majority of that at the lowest heart rate. He pointed to another heart-rate zone and said that for the next few months I should do the balance in this other zone.

Now I was armed. I felt like I had just had a lesson in nuclear physics. Lactate threshold, heart-rate zones, watts. I was armed and dangerous.

I then asked a question that I wished I had never asked. Sometimes ignorance is bliss. Sometimes it is better to let those around you talk laughingly about what a dope you are without proving it to them. Sometimes it is better to shut up and row. But I wanted to know how my lactate threshold stacked up against other fiftyish year-old men. He got a look on his face. The one that tells you that his explanation was going to be dose of reality that I may not want to hear. The look was enough to tell me all

I wanted to know. Clearly I sucked and only work could fix it. Slowly he explained the good news. No matter what the number was, it could be raised through training. He said that he had tested men over fifty with a threshold wattage of 270, but most of the good rowers were somewhere around 230.

I then asked another question I never should have asked. Much better to be stupid about things like this. The next question was, How long will it take me to get into the 230 watts area? His reply- two years minimum.

Thwup, thwup, thwup. About ten arrows went into my heart and lungs at once. Two years? I have to work like a dog for two whole years to get to point where I am in good enough shape to be called decent. How many thirty-minute pieces is that? Damn. My plan to become decent and slip away was crumbling. Damn, damn, damn. Right then I realized that to get in shape, I was going to have to commit to this sport at a level I had not anticipated.

This was essentially like a commitment to a varsity sport in school. Evenings, weekends. Ugh. Even if I just wanted to be mediocre required the same commitment, given where I was. Double ugh. This is what I get for having neglected my aerobic conditioning. This can't be done halfway.

As we drove home, I started to think about alternatives. As I learned in graduate school, there are always problems in a business, and working toward solutions is what separates great companies from weak ones. As I saw it, I had to solve the following problem: I had to lose weight and get in better shape. My eating habits were hard to improve. After all, I got on a train at five ten in the morning and got home at about eight p.m. I ate breakfast and lunch on the run but rarely consistently. Combined with travel and going out at night, eating was the hardest thing to control. Yes... I could eat better—more chicken and whole grains but less quantity. But beyond this effort, the idea of a controlled regular diet was probably not going to work. The alternative would be to increase the amount of regular exercise. Working out three to five times a week was probably doable. Long sessions were doable on the weekend. I did not relish coming home from work and hopping on an erg, but I did not have much of a choice if I was going to solve the problem.

The other alternative was the gym rat route: hole up in a gym several times a week doing elliptical, tread mill, stepper, and other such exercises. Not bad, but for what purpose? There is no competition between the athletes. There is no being on the water. There is no seeing the sun rise or set. There are no birds and other water life. There are no coaches yelling at you or encouraging you.

I had to make a commitment.

6

Work Hard, Finish Second

It was the start of the new Scott, soon to be super rower. First, I had to start a winter training program that made some sense. I asked Meredith what to do. She said that the club provides an outline of power, threshold, and low-cardio days but does not give specific workouts. Fine for my wife who's been through many years of winter training. But I had no clue how much low-cardio work to do, how much threshold or how much above threshold. My wife explained that there is also a periodization to your training. Periodization turns out to be the kinds of workouts you do in a certain sequence to produce optimal results.

It would have been easy to have just had Meredith design a plan, but there are always issues when husbands and wives do the same sport—like being each others coaches and ending up hating each other due to the better half's kind and helpful suggestions. So I started visiting websites with all sorts of suggestions. Concept2 (they make ergs—the rowing machines or medieval torture devices, depending on your mood) has training plans on their website. So I printed one. A website out of Canada that had a plan for the Canadian national team. There were training suggestions from PPOnline out of the UK. Xeno Muller, former singles Olympic champ, has a website with various workouts. There were all sorts of suggestions and websites. Like every other red blooded male, rather than ask for help with this mass of information, I basically guessed what would right for me.

I knew that I needed to do lots of exercise at lower heart rates (about 80 percent of the total volume) as was shown to me by Guenter. I also needed to work at higher heart rates. How high or how long I was not completely sure. The problem of assembling all this information is that everyone uses a different term and a different heart-rate target when talking about levels at which to train. One person's INE is another's CAT IV is another's lactate threshold. I also found that some sites described lactate threshold differently. So some would have you working at a lower heart rate than others and describe the purpose of the workout in a similar way.

Off I went, like trying to navigate New York City without knowing where you are going: clueless, not asking for help, trying to figure out what to do. I did the basic low-cardio. Then I did all manner of interval training, in which you do a series of shorter time frame erg pieces followed by a rest after each piece. For example, I would do seven three-minute erg pieces followed by three minutes of rest after each. The common shorthand for this is 7x3'. So I did 7x3', 10x2', 12x1', 5x5', 5x10'. I was the king of interval training. They were easy to whack out at night when I got home from work. I loved these things. I would even throw one-minute bursts into a low-cardio piece. To give you a picture, imagine a nice slow even paced low-cardio erg piece in which every few minutes you throw in a burst of fast intense rowing.

While the more experienced rowers are shaking their heads right now, I was sure I was becoming a rowing juggernaut. Like a good many novices I was sure I was training absolutely correctly. Any slight suggestions from Meredith would be met with disbelief, backed with the confidence of an article I had read. But I was a dope.

I rowed four to five days a week. I lifted weights on one of the rowing days and on one of the open days. When traveling I tried to stay in hotels that had ergs or access to them. Almost all hotels had weight rooms. I worked rowed, slept, went to work, and did it again.

All this work actually helped. I lost weight. I was losing a pound or two a month. I was sleeping better. I was actually feeling good. I cannot say that it was fun or that I looked forward to it. As a committed non-aerobic type, I am not sure I will ever say that I would love a twenty-minute race on the erg against your best buddy for the heck of it. I cannot say the same thing for a pick-up basketball game. But I was enjoying the results.

It went this way until January. During January, Concept2 sponsors a winter challenge in which clubs or groups band together to log all the meters they have erged. I decided that as the rookie, I was going to blow it out and try to row the most meters at our club. I stepped up my erging to six days a week when I could. On weekends I would sometimes do two sessions a day. I logged everything. Because I was one of the slower men on the erg, I figured I had to erg that much longer to make up for my lack of distance. I worked and worked. My back was sore, my butt was sore, but my life was focused. There were others at the club challenging my distances. I redoubled my efforts. On January 31, as the last meters were logged, I realized I was second.

I was disappointed but not too devastated. Many in the club now accepted me as committed. I was slow, not in great aerobic shape, and a crappy rower with whom no one wanted to row, but at least I had graduated from rookie to merely bad rower.

Being accepted as committed had other benefits. I was getting to know many of the people at the club. While I knew folks by name, I really had not created any relationships. As you erg, bike and lift next to folks, you slowly get to know them. You get to know what kind of sense of humor they possess. You get to know who are the committed, the somewhat committed and those that act committed but are not. You find out who likes whom.

I realized quickly that the club is like any other group of people. Everyone knows who is working hard and who is not. Everyone knows what everyone's erg times are. Everyone talks about who is improving and who is not working hard enough. Everyone gauges their progress off the progress of others. Some will say this is hyper-competitive. But it is really not. These are folks who love what they do and want to get better. Some of the club members have been successful at sports for an entire lifetime. Some have never done much sports-wise until rowing. And some should try a different sport- a category that probably includes me.

There is also a ritual at our club. After the Saturday and Sunday workouts, most members meet at a close restaurant called the Ocean View, nicknamed the OV, for breakfast. This is where the real action is. Club gossip is dispensed with relish. This is where you find out who is off to some camp, whose kids are driving them nuts, who has races against whom, who is honked off at one of the coaches, and who is happy or unhappy about rowing with whom.

So the club is a sort of community—it takes a village, Hillary—for getting better, for learning about how to compete, and for understanding what it takes to get to the next level.

7

Rowing Camp Redux

In February I decided to go the Florida Rowing Center, another of those rowing camps, for some training and to get away from the cold for a few days. I left from work for a three-day weekend in Wellington, Florida. I told Meredith that my goal was to graduate from tub to racing single, probably an ambitious goal given the amount of time I had on the water. But no guts no glory, I figured. After all, the worst that can happen is that you get a little wet with eighty-degree water in eighty-degree weather. So I packed my spandex shorts and off I went. I got on a plane after a day of work, arrived in Florida, and checked into my hotel room.

On the way to Florida, all I could think about was the amount of work we were going to be doing on the water for the next three days—two to three sessions a day. I was sure I'd be the worst rower there. The film sessions would be painful. The other rowers would look great. They'd be moving water aside when they rowed and have wakes coming off their boats. My boat would be the one with the slouched over troll with the belly—maybe I could keep the other rower goats from crossing a bridge as revenge for my bad form. My boat would be the one making so little progress that you could still fish off the back. Where is Scott? He was right there ten minutes ago. Yep, he is still there.

So, on the plane I formulated a plan. Like a prisoner facing lethal injection the next day, I decided to get the biggest, fattest, most disgusting form of red meat I could find for dinner. I was going to eat like an offensive tackle, and I was going to enjoy it. The next few days were going to be ego hammers. After I checked into the hotel, I asked where the best, close steak place was. I wrote down the name, called a cab, and had the cabbie escort me to my gourmand repast. A twenty-ounce strip accompanied by baked potato with sour cream and bacon was just the first course. It felt good to eat like a man again. No granola, no yogurt, no overage of green and leafy, no whole grains, no worry about the right balance of protein, carbohydrate and fat. No worry about the right fat. This was living! I could drown tomorrow in some freak rowing accident, and it would be okay. I was feted and feeling strong.

About an hour later, I felt like hell. Not from an overly full feeling, but just like crud. It was as if my body was rebelling. Rebelling from an old school meal that did not fit my more recent dietary habits. This can not be happening, I thought. Why me? Is this whole crunchy, happy, healthy lifestyle making my system repel this oh-so-good, awesome comfort food. I had to find some Tums or other such remedy. My body was in full rebellion.

To ease my pain and get my mind off my ailments, I called Meredith. I felt like a thirteen-year-old calling home after a couple of days at away camp. Mommy, I want to come home. I do not like it here. Everyone will make fun of me. People here are not very nice. The counselor is weird and says mean things. Thankfully, I did not whine. Just a quick I am here, and all is well, and we were off.

The next morning I pulled my spandex over my slightly larger gut, ate a Zone bar, and took the short drive to the rowing center. There I met my fellow campers before the coaches made their way down to organize the day. The coaches arrived, assigned boats, showed us the oars we'd be using, and told us to get in our boats. They indicated that the first row would be a filming and evaluation session. After this row we would have breakfast, watch our films, and return to the water to practice our instructional film updates.

I was an old hand now at getting the oars and the boat, a tub again, down to the water. I rigged the boat, attaching the oars to the oarlocks, crawled into the boat gingerly as always and pushed off the dock. I was one of the last ones off the dock, which was a positive as it cut down on number of people passing me. The coaches let us warm up and then started the filming. As they pulled near my boat to get the film, I remembered to sit up a bit, try to keep my knees together, and make it look like I had a clue. After all, I wanted to graduate to a racing single, a skinny boat. My film was quickly recorded, a few tips from the coach, and off they went to the next rower. We rowed for about an hour, came back to the dock, organized for breakfast and walked to a close restaurant.

Having learned my lesson from the night before, I ordered a yogurt, granola, and fruit parfait. Yummy. Marlene, one of the coaches, spent some time at breakfast querying me as to my goals of the session. I told her I wanted to row a skinny single and that I was tired of my wife being able to row circles around me. She asked if my wife's first initial was M!? I must have looked like I had been hit by lightning as she quickly responded that she did not know her. But she had seen her name showing up with some wins at regattas. Jeez. Not only is Meredith a better rower than me, she has a following. I was proud of her and the progress she had made, but now she was getting a reputation. Wow.

Marlene and I talked a bit more at breakfast. We talked about the sport, training, and the progress I was making. She was nice and nonjudgmental. She did let me know that my training could use some tweaking. She said that I was overtraining in the anaerobic zone, which would hurt me in the long run, and she suggested talking to my coach about it. Apparently, I needed more base training (low-cardio) and more threshold than I was doing. My base pieces were not long enough, and my threshold training was not designed properly. She suggested using Guenter's lactate threshold work as a base and to exercise off of the heart-rate ranges he showed me.

Marlene explained that two good workouts were thirty minutes of threshold and two twenty-minute threshold pieces. It is probably a good thing that I was not hooked up to an EEG at the time. The thought of a thirty-minute threshold piece did not really register. There would be no needles moving on that machine. Look, Doctor, a medical miracle. This guy is fully functional, but there is nothing going on up there. I was not doing thirty minutes of threshold in my current training, and it did not really register as being hard.

Unbelievably, I was feeling pretty good about the kind of aerobic training I needed and was wondering how I would work in these two twenty-minute threshold pieces. Then Marlene said it was time to go back to the rowing center for the film session. I knew this was going to be ugly. I was the most inexperienced rower in the group. I figured that when my film went up on the screen, most in the audience would get up and find something else to do. No use hanging around for this.

We went back to the film room and started. Just as in Craftsbury, everyone looked pretty good to me, but something strange happened. I was starting to notice a few mistakes other rowers were making. They all looked good, but I was beginning to see. Then it was my turn. Ugh. Sit up, lose weight, speed up were the thoughts that went through my head. As the video rolled I noticed I looked better than the previous film session. I got the usual comments about getting my oars in the water faster, my feather technique was weak, and my back should be straighter. But I got a compliment: I was told that I had nice balance. So I was a troll with balance. Now that is something. Another water session and we were done for the day.

The next morning was filled with anticipation for me. I wanted to graduate from the tub to a Peinert, a brand of boat used extensively for training purposes. I went to Marlene that morning and asked if I could try one. I am not sure that she knew how inexperienced I truly was. If she had know that I had been on the water less than fifteen times, she'd probably roll her eyes, laugh heartily, and tell me kindergarten graduation was a ways off. But she said okay and told me which boat to take. I took my oars down to the dock, then proudly grabbed the boat and put it in the water next to my oars. I put the oars into the oarlocks and crawled into the boat carefully. No problems so far. I could feel how much more unstable this boat was compared to the tub. I reached to my inside oarlock to make sure it was secure. No problems. I reached to outside oarlock. Huge problem. In my excitement to row this bad boy, I did not consider the balance issue. I reached out to check the oarlock and slowly rolled the boat right over.

As the boat rolled, all I could do was look to see who on the dock was having a laugh attack. Luckily, only a couple of folks were left. They helped me out of the water and to right the boat. They helped me into the boat and held the riggers so I would not roll again. I just wanted to get the hell out of there. But to do that, I would have to row this unstable beast. Taking a deep breath, I pushed away from the dock and quickly went into training-wheel mode. For the non-rowers, if you put your oars flat on top of the water while holding the handles for dear life, the boat sort of adjusts itself. I sat in this position for a few seconds to collect myself and figure out how I was going to pull this off.

I thought about all the things I had heard from other rowers: rushing the catch helps keep you more stable; using training wheels on the recovery to the next stroke helps keep you stable; shortening the stroke to half slide helps keep you more stable. So here we go, rushing a half-stoke and keeping my oars on the water during recovery. It was ugly, but I was rowing. After about one hundred yards I was able to lengthen the stroke a little. Little by little it got better. While no one watching would describe me as looking like a national team candidate, I was happy with the effort. The coach on the water motored by, gave me a few pointers and moved on. He was probably being kind, figuring it was just better to let me struggle through this mess.

I rowed to end of the lake and back, docked and went to breakfast with the others. After breakfast, it was back into the Peinert. No disasters. I was getting more comfortable. But I was already thinking about getting into an even more unstable boat the next day. I had come to Florida with the goal of getting into a racing boat, but after this day, I was not so sure. Should I just do the Peinert for another day? I went to my hotel that afternoon and tried to find all kinds of things to do to take my mind off the decision. I read, took a nap, went to dinner, and watched a movie. Finally sleep came at nine so I would not have to deal with the problem until the morning.

The next morning I got up, showered, pulled on the spandex and went to the rowing center. I decided on the way there while slurping up a Starbucks and eating a Zone bar that I was going to go for it. I was going to get in the boat and row. I was going to half slide, training wheel, and rush the catch until I did it. But when I got to the center I remembered one little item. What if the coach told me I needed more time in the Peinert? Go big or go home, I thought to myself. I went to the coach and asked which boat I should use. He asked me what I would like to try. I told him I wanted to try the Hudson. He pointed out the boat I should take to the dock.

It was that easy. Had he not seen me row? Certainly if he had, he would tell me to take the tub. Or maybe it was a conspiracy. They all wanted a good laugh while I flipped at the dock or on the water. Who is this guy? the coach probably thought. Why is he so full of himself? Let's have some fun with him.

I brought my oars and skinny, racing single to the water. As I rigged the boat, the thoughts of how skinny this boat looked were overwhelming. A mere twelve inches wide and about twenty-seven feet long. I had nailed pieces of wood together that were wider. All I could think of was that I was basically sitting on a buoyant, long two-by-four with a seat and shoes attached. I got in, pushed off, and went into protection mode—half-slide with training wheels. Surprisingly it was okay, though unstable. I was rowing this two-by-four, this thirty pound monster, a boat so delicate that a weak punch would go through its skin. My rowing was not pretty or fast. My oars stayed in training-wheel mode. And yes, I made it all around the lake without getting wet.

The boat felt different than anything I had rowed. It was lighter, more maneuverable. When you took a good stroke, it picked up the speed of the stroke. My form was bad, but when I hit a good stroke, the boat felt great. I was completely hooked. The boat responded to every twitch and instability I applied to it. This was really cool. I would not say that I had conquered rowing, but I had made an accommodation that allowed me to row this thing.

I rowed the loop and came back to the dock. I had to fly home in a few hours so I gathered my things, thanked the coaches and drove back to hotel.

I was firmly on cloud nine. What an awesome feeling. I could only imagine what it would be like if I could row well. I called Meredith excitedly and told her I had done it and it was awesome. I did not care if I could be better, if I was off balance most of the time, or if I had the training wheels down. What an awesome row. It was probably a good thing that I had to buckle my seat belt on the plane. I was so excited I might have been bouncing around on the ceiling. As I flew home strapped into my seat, I decided to buy a single.

8

Shelling Out the Dough

I would like to believe that I am a rational person. I would like to believe that when I make a decision that all sides of the decision are weighed, measured, calculated, and considered. I would like to believe that when someone asks me why I made that decision, I reply with a clarity of logic that renders the decision to little scrutiny. Unfortunately, this cannot be said about my decision to buy a single.

As a matter of course, this may have been the most emotional decision I've ever made. I had rowed a racing single once. I had never participated in a race. My rowing skill was nil. While buying a single for a beginner is somewhat idiotic, buying it in the winter is completely ignorant.

Most people row several boats before deciding which single to buy. They will row boats from Italian, German, Canadian, and American makers. Most people have some sense of the differences in boats at the beginning of the process given that they have been in a number of different quads, doubles, and eights. After the initial trial, most people go back and row their top two or three choices again to figure out which they like. Some rowers will like the catch of certain boats, some will like the run on other boats. Most people have studied the construction of the boat and understand which boat has a decent reputation for quality, service, and ease of maintenance.

None of this describes my decision. After returning from Florida, I told Meredith that I wanted to buy a single. I will give her credit. She pulled hard on the reins of my horses and tried to slow my decision. She valiantly attempted to tell me the downside of what I was attempting to do. But she failed miserably.

After Florida, I did my usual research of the boat makers: I went online. I learned that the amount of the boat that touches the water when you row, called wetted surface, has the largest influence on the speed of the boat. The less wetted surface the better. I also learned that the bow wave is the other big determinant of speed. Do not ask me what this means or how you measure it, but I learned that it's important. Finally, I learned that the amount of deflection of the sides of the boat influences the power of oars. So basically, as you pull on the oars, the less the boat sides move with that power application, the more power goes through the oars into the water.

Now that I understood the physics, I was ready. I read all the boat-makers' websites. I learned some boats are all carbon fiber. Some boats have carbon fiber and Kevlar. Some boats have carbon fiber with a core or some sort sandwiched between the carbon fiber. Some boats weighed more than others by a couple of pounds. A couple of pounds may not seem like a lot. But when a boat weighs only twenty-eight or thirty pounds, a couple of pounds seemed like a lot. This knowledge, though, did not help me at all. I was aware of the differences in the boats, but was not sure if it made one boat better than another.

I asked Meredith what boats she liked to row. I asked her if she liked that yellow German single of hers. I asked what she would do. Her answer was to wait. But I was not to be deterred. I was a man on a mission. I began to call the boat manufacturers.

I tried to ask informed questions about the quality of their construction and the reasons they used some materials over others. I had the feeling that when I had hung up, the person on the other side of the call was wondering when I had been let out of the asylum.

After all this work, which yielded little true understanding, I bought a boat. A boat I had never rowed. A boat I had only seen pictures of Xeno Muller (the single winner in the 1996 Olympics and a silver medalist in 2000) carrying on his shoulder. A boat that I would not be able to row for months. I had bought a boat the coaches would not even let me in until the water warmed in the late spring. I had bought a boat that I would not be able to row until the coaches felt comfortable enough with my rowing ability. I bought a boat after having been in a racing single once in my life. This decision was the equivalent of buying your child a turbo Porsche before obtaining a learner's permit.

And how did I decide to buy this boat? I liked the people of the other end of the phone. It basically came down to marketing 101: customer service matters. I bought a single made by Kaschper, a Canadian manufacturer. When I had called the company, a woman fielded my technical questions, a few for which she said she'd get answers. Sure enough, I received a long e-mail for Mr. Kaschper himself, explaining all the reasons he made boats the way he did and the implications for their performance. He should have e-mailed it to the baboon cage at the Bronx Zoo, as I understood little of the technical info. But the effort was appreciated.

So... I wrote a check and mailed it to Canada. I am not known for being a spender. I am still amazed that after one row in a skinny single, I was more than willing to write a check.

As I look back on this decision, I am most taken by what the purchase represented. Only a few months before, I came to this sport with not the best of attitudes. I was destined to be a rowing casualty. I was slated to be one of those folks who shows up a few times, realizes the amount of work involved, and heads to a less demanding regimen of the stair stepper and elliptical. The decision was a commitment to the sport.

I started this sport with less than good intentions. I had wanted merely to quiet all those who wanted me to get into better shape. While I knew they were right, I was not that committed to the process. But as I rowed, erged, and lifted, I was becoming a convert. It was a subtle conversion. I did not just wake up and say I am ready to row. Actually, I cannot say that to this day I actually look forward to the workouts. This may sound weird, but watch college swimmers as they prepare to get into the water for a workout. They seem to delay the process of getting into the water forever. They splash water on themselves. They put water on their goggles. They will adjust their hat and goggles ten times. They make sure everything fits right, like it really matters for a workout. After an eternity, they jump in. Even then, some will mess with this or that before they begin.

This scenario describes me when it comes to workouts. I do not look forward to them, but once I start, I am committed. But starting is tough. Many at the club are Sponge Bob rowers: They say nice things—what a great workout; what a great day; we had nice water today; you guys looked great. I am not that way. I just want to get my workout done and over with. I do not look forward to starting the workout. I would mess around on the dock for half an hour if the coaches were not yelling for us to clear the dock for other rowers. But even with my less than upbeat attitude, I was doing the work. And as much as I did not look forward to the workouts, I did not want to miss any. If I was out of town or had some evening event to attend, I would make up the missed workout within a few days.

The hard work was paying off. I was shedding weight. Pants that did not fit six months before were easy to get on. Going up and down stairs was less of an effort. The long hours at work did not seem so long. Sleep came quickly at night. I felt better and less tired during the day. Did my kids notice? Nah. They are kids. Dad is Dad. They hate the spandex and beg me to change as soon as I get home. It could be embarrassing if one of their friends saw me.

If I'd have bet a year before about me doing this kind of exercise, I would have lost that bet. When I first started rowing, the idea of being on a stationary bike or elliptical seemed like one of the biggest bores in the world. I do not think I had ever lasted for more than fifteen minutes on one of these machines before. Now I was using them for hours a couple of times a week in an effort to cross-train for my low-cardio work. Not only that, but I was beginning to be one of those erg peekers. The ergs have a timer on them that allows you to see the splits, watts, and distances you are rowing. All rowers silently check on others to see how they are stacking up. What is rower X doing today? Oh no, he is pulling a threshold piece at a 1:52 split for thirty minutes. I had better get to work.

9

Back to the Grind

I returned to the training regimen after the trip home and my less-than-informed boat purchase. Another month to six weeks of hard training was ahead before we could get back on the water. At least a month of sweating indoors. At least a month of lifting weights. Marlene from the Florida Rowing Center put together a training program for me. I was clearly clueless about what to do for my training, judging from my conversation with her. Reading the websites, doing lactic acid test, and whacking away on various pieces of cardio equipment had not helped me learn much.

The first thing Marlene required was to do a number of different tests during a week. I had to do a thirty-second erg piece, going as hard as I could and recording the max watts pulled. Then she had me row as hard as I could for seventy-five minutes. Also I was to do a thousand-meter race, and finally I rowed for twenty minutes all out. I spent a week getting all this done. After I sent Marlene the results, she came back with a three-hundred-page plan. She covered everything from my personal aerobic training plan to weight-lifting routines to stretching routines with copious pictures and descriptions.

As I read through the plan, I was surprised by two things. One was the amount of aerobic work that was involved. The second was the weight-lifting routines that I have now learned are common to rowing. The routines were broken down into power, strength, and strength endurance. I laughed cynically at all this when I read it. I knew how to lift. All guys have lifted weights at some point in our athletic career. All coaches would have a super-sized program for you that promised incredible results. The power and the strength workouts I understood; they were similar to other workouts I had done. *Power* was lots of Olympic moves. Cleans, dead pulls, snatches, squats and the like for a short amount of reps and a bunch of sets. The moves are performed as fast as you could and still maintain your form. *Strength* was the traditional moderate number of reps done in several sets. The strength endurance work is the one that to this day I do not get. How does doing sixty to eighty squats or bench presses or high pulls with low weight help that much? When you row, aren't you doing strength endurance? Someone please tell.

The aerobic work was broken down with terminology used by the training program I found for the Canadian national team. The workout intensity was broken down into categories (CAT for short) II, III, IV, V, and VI. Why the Roman numerals? I dunno. Wouldn't it have been easier for the truly aerobically challenged and mentally slow, like me, to use regular numbers? CAT II was race pace while CAT III was just slightly below. CAT IV was threshold. CAT V and VI were low-cardio workouts. Low-cardio meant they were somewhat easy, with VI being the easiest (*easy* meaning that you can train at that level for long periods). Trust me though—sweating profusely is still part of the workout.

To say I was surprised by the amount of work involved in Marlene's plan is a vast understatement. I was sure that she had sent me a plan for someone trying out for the national team. Two hours of CAT VI one day a week. One hour at CAT IV. That has to be a joke. I had never done anywhere near that amount continuously. Her definition of CAT IV required a much faster split time than I was doing currently. And what is this *hour* BS? This was hard. Her basic plan was three days of CAT VI, one day of CAT V, and two days of CAT IV. Within this framework there was some CAT III thrown in from time to time. Throw three days of weight workouts on top of all this, and we had a plan.

So I tackled her plan for about a month. I sweat, breathed hard, and swore at Marlene. I could not believe how incredibly hard it was. I was whipped and doing it at night after work was the worst. I would get home at eight o'clock or so, get a little to eat, and change into workout clothes. I would go downstairs, flip the TV on, get on the erg and begin the sweat-a-thon.

After the workout, it was back upstairs to finish dinner. Then a quick shower was followed by bed. I was tired and hungry all the time. Thankfully, it only lasted a little longer than a month, as we were starting to get back on the water again. My loving wife suggested that we make another trip to Guenter to see what progress we had made in winter training. After the last trip's ego bomb, I was not excited. I reasoned that I was in better shape but that Meredith's numbers would still be better than mine. But why go and prove it to be true?

Over my feeble objections and vain attempts at weaseling out of the trip, off we went one Saturday to see the lactic acid king, Guenter. He had us both doing our test at about the same time. At the end of our tests he went to read the blood sample stats and produce the results. He was smiling when he gave Meredith her results. He told her that she was doing very well. That she was at very high levels of threshold. Then came my turn.

He handed me my stats and said I had improved. He asked me how much work I was doing. I was not quick to tell him. I hesitated, wondering if I should embellish the truth. He had asked an open-ended question. Open-ended questions usually have bad news attached to them. Nobody ever asks an open-ended question to give you good news. It is always, "Do you eat a lot of butter?" You answer, "I really like it, but I do not eat a lot." They say- "Gee, too bad. You are going to have to quit eating it altogether. I am not sure how you are living now given your blood pressure." Watch out for the open-ended question. Do not answer them. They are traps.

With my hesitation, Meredith stepped in and said something about how much work I was doing. Guenter said that was good. He said that when I came in the fall, I clearly had a ton of work to do. Thanks, Guenter. Let's rub it in. He said I had improved but still had a way to go given the level at which I started. There was no congrats as there had been for Meredith. There was no "you are getting close to your goals." Nope… the finish line was still a long way away. I did not ask him this time how long this was going to take. I already knew the answer: for freaking ever.

10

Splish Splash

I cannot say that I was unhappy when after about a month of the winter training program, it was time to get back on the water for the club workouts. You might wonder why I could not pursue Marlene's training program on the water as well. After all, her program was easily transferable to a water workout. When on the water, a rower is faced by two issues. First, unless you are in a single, you have rowing partners with whom you have to work. None of them were on my plan, so there is no incentive to do the same work as me. Secondly, there is a coach telling us what our workout is for the day. Ignoring the workout can lead the coaches to think you have little interest in learning what they have to teach. Because I was such a bad rower, I needed all the coaching help I could get. So Marlene's training plan went out the window. It was probably a good thing, though. After a month of her training plan I was imagining Marlene as some sort of iron maiden who enjoyed seeing men in pain.

In return I was greeted with the following weekly cycle:

Monday- off day

Tuesday- Power, typically hard rowing for 10 to 30 strokes followed by a similar rest period. When in doubles or quads, only half the boat rows at any one time to make it harder.

Wednesday- Threshold, typically 10 minute pieces done 4 to 6 times with 5 minutes of rest in between.

Thursday- Low-cardio, a long row at about 70-75 % of your maximum heart rate

Friday- Power again

Saturday- Threshold. Saturday was called race day. This is when we did two 5000-meter pieces. These days were reasonably competitive and most of us went over our threshold levels during the workout since times were recorded. We all wanted to have a reasonable time.

Sunday- Low-cardio

As we started on the water, I worked faithfully within the parameters given to me, whether on the water or on the erg. At this point most of the rowers knew me. They spoke to me but still considered me less than good. I was put in boats by the coaches, probably over the objections of those with whom I was rowing. I was not aware of any overt attempts to keep me out of any boat. But the signals from the other rowers were unmistakable. Besides the normal jovial rookie ribbing, I heard comments from the other rowers: "You are splashing," "get your blades in faster," "you are rushing the slide," "do not drop your elbows at the finish," and "the boat is not set." These comments probably mean nothing to the non-rower. But to the rower, the others in the boat were sending signals to me that I had issues. Translation for these comments is as follows:

You are splashing: Recall that in rowing, when you take your blades out of the water at the finish of the stroke, you "feather" or rotate them so the flat side of the blade is parallel to the water. So to put the blade back into the water, you have to rotate them back to perpendicular. If you do this rotation too close to the water, you will flick water onto the person behind you. Since the water temperature is somewhere in the high 40 to low 50 degree area in the early part of the season, drenching a person with bad rowing form is not appreciated. It also slows down the boat. Therefore, you get the double whammy—people get wet and you slow down the boat.

Get your blades in the water faster: A rower can only move the boat when the oars are in the water. If you do not get your blades in at the same time everyone else does, you are handing the boat to all the other rowers for the early part of the stroke. This technique not only slows the boat but makes your partners work harder. Do not do this if you want a happy boat.

You are rushing the slide: Remember that the seats slide on these boats. At the finish of the stroke when you take the blades out of the water, your legs are at full extension. So you have to pull yourself back to a compressed position, at which point you put the blades back into the water. While you are moving to a compressed position, you are not moving the boats but letting the power of the previous stroke glide the boat along. As a beginner, the natural tendency is to try to rush the seat slide to compressed position so you can take another stroke and power up the boat. It is almost like you are a one cylinder engine; the faster you can make that cylinder cycle, the faster you will be. The problem is that this can interfere with the glide of the boat, also called the run of the boat. During this portion of the stroke, the rower is trying to get compressed and is pulling themselves into the stern of the boat. This movement is opposite the direction that you want the boat to move. So the idea is to interfere with the run of the boat as little as possible. Somebody, somewhere figured out that there is a ratio that works best for this timing and that simply rushing up the slide and slamming your oars into the water makes you slower. When another rower in your boat tells you to stop rushing the slide, he or she is saying you are moving up to the compressed position too fast and are screwing up the speed of the boat. Another phenomenon occurs when a rower is rushing the slide, called whiplash. When a rower's slide is out of sync with others in the boat, the out of sync rower is creating inertia in the boat and causing the other rowers to feel themselves being slammed into the compression at the catch. This also slows down the boat.

Do not drop your elbows at the finish: At the finish the rower has to extract the oar blades from the water quickly and cleanly. Think of it as trying to pull a knife from a stick of butter while the stick of butter is moving away from you. The rower wants to perform this extraction in a manner that disturbs the butter as little a possible so as not to slow the travel of the butter. When a rower drops the elbows at the finish, the blades are hard to extract from the water and you tend to feather the blades in the water. Feathering in the water slows the boat.

The boat is unset: This means that the boat is either leaning to the right or left or is rocking back and forth. It is very hard to get the oars in and out of the water consistently if the boat is not set. Also the more the boat rocks, the slower it is. There is a fin (skeg) on the bottom of the boat. If the boat is moving side to side, the skeg is creating resistance against the water and slowing down the boat.

Hearing all this as a rower means you that you basically stink and have a lot to work on. Well, I was hearing this stuff a lot both from the coaches and other rowers in my boat. It was late March and unless I was placed in a boat by the coaches, I do not think anyone would have rowed with me. Usually the coaches liked to put rowers of similar skill in the same boat and let them struggle and learn together. Unfortunately, there were not any other rowers at the time with my complete lack of talent.

Despite all the frustration that comes with the learning to row with others, I persevered. I cannot think of any other word that describes the process. Rowing is hard work. It is a cardio-based sport filled with adults who are committed to getting better and work hard to do it. To start anew at this sport is as much of a motivational challenge as it is a physical challenge.

For the next month I went to the club as often as I could to be placed in boats. I listened to all the things I was doing wrong and worked to improve. When I could not make it to the club, I erged and lifted weights. Much like golf where the accumulation of swings makes you better, rowing requires a large amount of strokes to see improvement. Slowly but surely, the coaches and other rowers were telling me less. And when there was an instructional point, I understood better how to move the boat more effectively. Not that I was fast; I was just less clueless. Or at least, so I thought. More likely, everyone was just tired of telling me the same stuff over and over.

Slowly, I was placed into more and different boats, which I interpreted as an indication that I was improving. Maybe I had just worn out my welcome in the other boats. But on one of those days I was placed into a double with a fellow named Ed. We had rowed in a quad but had never rowed a double together. We were told to use a boat called the school bus, a yellow early 2000s Hudson double. It was the first time I had been allowed to row that boat. I was excited at being allowed to row a better boat, but I doubted it was because of my skill. It was probably because Ed would be bowing.

The bow rower is responsible for making the calls to the crew, Ed and me in this instance. The calls let the other rowers know what to do. The bow will call starboard or port and the crew will pull harder on the called side to turn the boat where it needs to go. Since Ed had many years of rowing experience, I assumed that the coaches were comfortable with his ability to guide me down the river without hurting the boat.

Some will read this as the coaches being more worried about the boat than the rower. That is not the implication that I want to leave. These boats are light and delicate. A good double weighs somewhere around sixty pounds and is around twenty-eight feet long. A boat that big and light has to be delicate. While the coaches worry about our safety, they also worry about a ten-thousand-dollar-plus investment in a boat.

Also while we are on this subject, I can hear my football-playing friends roll their eyes at the thought of pushing a sixty pound object up and down a river. I am sure many are wondering just how hard that can be. After all, my son, who played football in college, could curl a sixty-pound weight with one arm without too much effort. What most forget is that you are pushing the boat plus the weight of the rowers over distances in excess of a mile. So in the case of Ed and me, the two of us are pushing a sixty-pound boat plus a total weight of around four hundred pounds in races that last between four and twenty minutes. Add to that the balance and form issues of moving a boat efficiently. No Mr. Ex-linebacker, it is not the same as going mano y mano with a 280-pound lineman, and you do not need the same strength. But in terms of the kind of shape you need to be in to do this sport at a competitive level, it is sort of like pushing a full wheel barrow as fast as you can for a long time.

Ed and I pushed off the dock. I am sure Ed was worried about my ability, given my short rowing resume. I tried hard not to suck as we went through our warm-up drills and rowed up the river. Thankfully for us, but probably especially thankfully for Ed, today was a low-cardio day. This meant we would be doing lower stroke rates (somewhere around twenty strokes per minute) with our heart rates in the 130s. This was easier to coordinate for me as a beginning rower and easier for Ed to follow my inconsistent stroke. The goal in any multiple-rower boat is to coordinate our efforts to move the boat efficiently. This means that we have to be almost mirror images of each other. As I was rowing stroke, the person in the stern seat, Ed's job would be to guide us down the river and follow my inconsistent lead. With my rookie status and inconsistent stroke, I was focused on making his job easy by trying to row in a reasonably non-rookie manner. Somehow or another we ended rowing about 12,000 meters that day without too many bad strokes—a testament to Ed's ability to follow my poor lead.

At the end of the row, Ed thanked me and said he would like to row again. I put the comment down to pure gentlemanliness and doubted that he would go out of his way to row with me again. It was nice of him to say but given his experience, I figured I was sort a "mercy" row and that was that. I figured Ed would be hiding the next few times rowers were assigned to boats until I had been assigned to my boat. Oly oly oxenfree. You can come out now, Ed. The coaches have assigned Scott to a boat.

As the weather slowly warmed, the water warmed with it. When the water was in the high fifty- to low sixty-degree range, the coaches allowed me to row a single again. I had not rowed a single since the Florida Rowing Center in February. The coaches were reluctant to let someone with my limited skills be on the water until the risk of hypothermia had subsided, in the event of a flip. The coaches finally gave in to my many appeals and allowed me to go out in a Peinert. As predicted, they wouldn't let me anywhere near my shiny new boat until I had proven myself.

On the morning of that fateful day, I had a coach help me guide the boat down to the water. We put the boat in while I placed my water bottle by my foot stretcher and put the oars into the proper places. I eased my stiff morning body into the single and was about to push off when I was yelled at in Russian English to hold up for a second. As I sat in place next to the dock, one of the coaches ran down with a bright orange life preserver and stuffed it in the boat.

What infamy! What shame! Might as well hang a huge sign around me identifying me as a rookie. I sat for a second composing myself from the insult to my ability and then slowly pushed off the dock. To say that the extra month or so of rowing on the water after the end of winter training had improved my ability to row a single would be a gross overstatement. The damned boat felt like crud to me, like I was back at the Florida Rowing Center. Everything felt unstable. The mere act of sitting on the water was uncomfortable. I began at about half stroke (taking half of a stroke) and probably did it for the better part of my row. When I did go to some semblance of a full stroke, I rushed the stroke badly, trying to get the oars in the water as fast as possible to offset the instability that a slow and measured stroke would give me. I was just terrible. Thankfully the coaches were busy with other rowers and watched me from afar to make sure that I did not go for a swim. After rowing a short distance that took way too long to accomplish, I came back to the dock. I clumsily got out of the boat. Nobody would confuse me with the word graceful. I took the boat to the wash rack, cleaned it up and put it away. I humbly dragged my butt home.

Those with experience will say it takes time to be comfortable in a skinny single. There are people who have rowed in big boats for years and do not tackle the skinny single. I had been on the water for maybe three months total. What the hell do you expect?

Looking back on it now, I imagine that I was just tired of the rookie status. As my single rowing ability was shown to all watching as weak, it was then that I decided that I would row the single as much as possible. I reasoned that the instability of the single would help me be a better rower. I imagined that the unstable platform would better help me understand when I was correctly and incorrectly applying power to the oars. I figured that if I stank in a single, I probably stank in bigger boats. But the stability of the bigger boat was just masking my poor rowing. From now on I would work on the single a lot.

A few days after making this commitment, rower Ed returned to the boathouse and asked me if I would like to do a double again. I hope I did not look to dumbstruck when he asked. I thought our row had gone well, but I had not really thought that he would share that feeling. In any event we ventured out again in what would become a three-times-a- week rowing affair. We rowed on Tuesday, Thursday, and Saturday when we were both available. We worked hard, and I enjoyed having a regular row. Every once in a while someone would slip and say something nice like, "You guys are doing well." Of course my inner skeptic would take over and interpret that statement to mean, "You guys are doing well given the handicap of having Scott, the lard ass, in the boat."

Despite my thorny personality and rowing incompetence, Ed continued to row with me. Several days a week we would meet at the club and do the prescribed workout torture. I found that having a consistent partner became a luxury. You know what to expect and what to work on. We even started talking about what races we should consider doing. As we spoke about doing races, I was optimistic. I was sure that we would fare reasonably well. Certainly all the work I had done over the winter and for the first fifty days on the water would yield positive results. Our double was beating several of the women's quads on Saturday race day. So certainly we were somewhat competitive.

We agreed that our first race would be Derby, held on the Housatonic River in Shelton, Connecticut, and sponsored by the New Haven Rowing Club. We agreed to sign up for a double. The race was about three weeks. There was also a novice single race, for master rowers who have been rowing less than a year. That description was perfect for me. I assumed I even had a chance at finishing well in that race. We were also told by the coaches that Ed and I would be included in a quad that day.

In the time that was left leading up to the race, Ed and I worked out a few issues. First, we had never done a start together. This may seem like a small issue. But in a thousand-meter sprint race like Derby, your start is important. Getting out in front or staying with the pack allows you to see what your competitors are doing. Unlike a foot race in which running behind the leader can be an advantage, in rowing you are facing backward. Therefore it helps to get ahead or at least be in the pack of boats so you can see what the other rowers are up to. Are they dying?

Are they gaining or losing ground on you? All are important questions if you have competitive instincts.

Secondly, Ed and I had never really rowed more than 28 strokes per minute. I was not all that comfortable at high stroke rates. We had to get some practice in. I asked Meredith what SPM she and her doubles partner were doing in races. She said it varied from 32 to 34, depending on race conditions, where they were in the pack, how the boat felt, and other factors.

Four more SPM did not seem undoable. Ed and I decided to work on our starts at least once a week. We also decided that we would row part of our workouts at a high SPM.

On our next Tuesday row we used part of the time to work on starts. We talked through what we would be doing. We would start at the catch, that is, fully compressed, and begin to row from a dead stop. Ed said that most boats have a cadence that they use to get the boat moving. So the first stroke might be a half stroke, followed by a three-quarter stroke, next another half stroke, then a three-quarter stroke, and begin to lengthen from there. He also indicated that we want to take these strokes as fast as we can, upwards of forty SPM. I told him I had no clue what cadence to use, so he could make the call. We decided to try a half, three-quarter, three-quarter, half, and lengthen.

Ed made the call as the starter would:

Ready (move up to the compressed position with your feathered oars on the water for stability).

Attention (square up the blades and put them in the water).

Row (begin your start).

Off we went. On the first stroke I completely skipped out, meaning that my oars did not stay in the water for the full half stroke we were attempting. It also caused me to come down heavily in the boat. Both of these slowed the boat. On the second stroke I rushed the slide and got my oars in the water ahead of Ed. Another speed killer. On the third, I just went lights out and forgot that we were attempting a three-quarter stroke and just started lengthening. Not a killer, but hard for Ed to follow since he was not expecting it. We did a fourth and a fifth that were probably just as bad as the first three. I guess after five or six strokes Ed had participated in enough fun. He called "weigh enough," rower lingo for stop.

Ed nicely said that we had work to do. Ed is the master of understatement. We tried several more cadences before settling on half, half, three-quarter, three-quarter, and begin to lengthen. This type of start is just basically starting short and getting longer. Pretty simple and not a lot for dopey rower Scott to remember. We worked on this a few more times and then went on to our regular workout. We did this start sequence each week, practicing it several times each session until the race. Poor strokes, buried oars, poor timing, and other issues were worked out. Sort of.

We also had to work on rowing at higher SPM. We agreed that we seem to move the boat best at a 26 SPM. Clearly, we had work to do to get to 30 during the three weeks before the race. We started by inserting one-minute pieces at 30 SPM. At every row we do a couple of these pieces. The next week we moved it up to two minutes at 30 SPM. In the final week we tried to do 32 SPM for a minute. A couple of times we hit 33 SPM, but we could not hold it for the entire minute. On top of this we were pretty whipped after a minute or two at this rate.

Despite our less than Olympic starts and high stroke rate dysfunction, I was reasonably positive about what our performance would look like. I figured we were in reasonable shape and had reasonable skills and were awfully nice people. Therefore, we should be modestly triumphant. I say this without knowing Ed's thoughts. He probably thought that he was in rowing disasters 101. In addition to the doubles race, I had a singles race that I was focusing on. I figured that my doubles start practice would be enough practice for the single start. But I did some high-stroke rate work in the single.

High stoke rates in the single were typically accompanied by a lot of splashing, shortened strokes in an effort to keep the boat balanced, and huge ungainly catches. My strokes looked like a helicopter spinning toward earth completely out of control. I was also burying the blades a lot, according to coaches. This means that the oars were going deeper than they should. When you get your blades too deep you are lifting the boat off the water a bit with each stroke. The rower should be gliding across the water with each stroke. Lifting the boat wears you out quickly and slows you down—clearly not optimal.

Despite all my issues, I figured it was a novice race so everyone would be as bad as me. As the race approached, I felt nervous but excited to display my exemplary skills on the water.

11

Flailure

On Friday, the day before the race, members of the club derigged boats and put them on a trailer for transport to the regatta. Derigging involves removing the superstructure that supports the oarlocks off the boat. This leaves just the shell, which is easier to transport. We strapped the boats to the trailer and nervously waited for Saturday to greet us. Meredith spent the evening playing down the race. She can get nervous before a race, so I knew it was best not to ask her too many questions. Looking back maybe it was not her nerves that were the issue. Perhaps she knew that a rookie's first race is full of potential issues. Maybe she knew that a Keystone cop performance was a possibility, and she did not want me to get too nervous about rookie mishaps. At the time I was sure it was her problem, not mine.

At about six thirty we left the house for the forty-minute ride to the race. Meredith had an early race and wanted to get to the site to rig her boat. We got up early threw everything we needed into the back end of the Suburban—lunches, chairs, slings to hold the boats for rigging, water, rigging tools, rigging for the singles and her double, wallets, extra clothes, suntan lotion, and replacements for just about anything that could break or be lost. We looked like we were taking a family trip to Montana, like *National Lampoon's Vacation.* All we needed was Chevy Chase to complete the scene.

We arrived at the race to the sight of hundreds of rowers and coaches, all rigging boats up. We parked and made several trips to our club's trailer to dump our belongings. Meredith and I both rigged our singles, since the singles races were the first of the day.

I spent time trying to assuage my nerves by helping others. Better to keep busy than to think about the race. Thankfully, Meredith's race was first. I helped her with her boat, walking it to the river with her. She got in, received a couple of reminders from the coach, and began to go through her warm up on the way to the start. Twenty or thirty minutes later, her race began.

Now, it may seem that in the years Meredith had been rowing, I would have seen her row at least once. Not so. Weekend child duties always seemed to get in the way. I had never seen her race before, so I was interested in watching.

One of things I quickly noticed is that you really have no idea when an individual race begins. We were at the finish line watching a race that started a thousand meters down the river. While I am not too blind, it is difficult to figure out who is whom at that distance. Also, there are no announcements. Races start, and at about 300 to 400 meters, you can begin to tell if a particular person is in that race. I stood by the coaches and asked them to poke me when they saw Meredith.

After about twenty minutes, she appeared and rowed to the finish. She was first in her race. Very exciting. Unfortunately my race was not far away at this point. When she got to the shore line and hauled her boat back to the trailer, she said we should take my boat down to the water so I could warm up on the way to the start. Butterflies began to appear. We put her boat away and took mine to the water. I put the oars in the oarlocks and got in. Meredith asked what warm-up I was doing. I said I thought

I would just row to the start and received the "you're not too smart" smile.

Rower wife said I should do some high stroke rates for a few minutes to get the heart pumping. She said there will be a line of people in races ahead of mine, and I would not be able to just row to the start. I should just slot into the lineup when I got down there. She told me to look for a particular rower who was in the race ahead of mine and try to fall in somewhere behind that person. Okay.

This is all the instruction I had about how to do a race. Here I am, the rawest of the raw, with a quick couple of instructions before the race on what to do. It seems that no one really gets any guidance at their first race. Books could be written about first race pratfalls. I was thankful for a rowing spouse, as I am not sure that I would have gotten any advice at all before the race. Was this some kind of test? If you cannot figure out what to do, then you will not be invited back. If you are too stupid just to row off and attempt this without actually sitting down with someone to figure out how to accomplish it, then you must be too stupid to row. I guess I was almost too stupid to row. Thank you, wife, for bailing me out.

I rowed off. About a hundred yards down the river I heard someone screaming at me to move over. Move over to where. The race was on my right coming up the river and I was on the left going down the river. Where in God's name was I supposed to go? Suddenly, my fin (skeg) on the boat hit bottom. Since the skeg is only extends six inches below the bottom of the boat, I had gotten myself in pretty shallow water and needed to row into a deeper part of the river. That's why I was being yelled at. Sheepishly, I scraped my way to a deeper part of the river.

Southerners Do Not Row

Now that I had completely screwed up the first hundred yards of my row, I figured it was time to recover and think about what I needed to do for the warm-up. I decided to do one minute of fast rowing and one minute of slow rowing continuously down the river to the start. Unfortunately after about six minutes I was at the start. Not much of a warm-up. I stopped and turned around in the boat to see where to slot in. I saw a line of boats that extended for two-hundred yards down the river. Boats were strung out everywhere. I thought about a sign the high school team had hanging in the boathouse: "Shut up and Row." So that is exactly what I did, looking for the one recognizable face in that mass of carbon fiber and flesh to fall in behind. I had been warned by someone not to row too far past the warning buoys about 500 meters downriver from the start. There was a waterfall there. So I rowed and kept an eye for a face and an eye for the warning buoys behind me. I finally saw the face I was looking for and slotted into the lineup behind him.

As I got into the lineup, other rowers began asking what race I was in. I thought this was just a friendly act, but I soon realized that the rowers were also trying to figure out where to slot in. We slowly rowed back up river to the start as the races went off. Finally it was time for my race. The starter called for all men's novice racers. Three of us started rowing to the start. I was in lane 4 and two other boats were in lanes 3 and 1. When we got to the line, the starter began to line us up.

Lane 4, take a stroke.
Lane 3, hold.
Lane 1, back row one stroke.

I was in trouble. Please do not ask me to back row, I thought. Back rowing requires a little description. Back rowing is called that because that's what it would look like from shore. But since you face backward, it is really, from a rower's point of view, front rowing. Unless you practice it occasionally, it is fraught with potential disaster for the new rower. First you have to feather your blades the wrong way so that the cup of the blade faces toward the water. This means that it is very easy to catch a blade by accident and flip. Secondly, the whole stroke is reversed, which for the new rower requires a bit of rowing stroke deconstruction. It is not something that I wanted to do on the verge of my first nervous race start.

So I completely wimped. When the starter told me to take another stroke, I probably only moved the boat a foot or so. He called for another stroke, and another. I inched my way to even with the other rowers.

Suddenly he called

Ready.

I looked at the other rowers as they came to the compressed position. I did the same.

Attention

The other two rowers feathered their blades to square and put their oars in the water. Again, I did the same. Hells bells. Please start this race. This is a pretty unstable position.

Row

They were off, and I was sort of off. In my vain attempt to start my single, I dug an oar and almost flipped. I reorganized and tried again, this time with less power, and I was off slowly.

It would be nice to say that despite being seriously behind at the start, I closed the distance and had a race on my hands. That would be inaccurate. I started slow and finished slower. At the finish I was thirty seconds behind the number two boat, which was fifteen seconds behind the number one boat. I had no idea how hard to pull or how hard to go. I just sort did what seemed best, and clearly that was not hard enough. I doubt I could have won, but I think I could have been a lot faster. To give you a frame of reference, when they posted the times of all the singles races, I was the slowest rower in the entire field. I was slower than seventy-year-old men and women. I was slower than forty-year-old women who could not curl ten pounds. I was a mess.

Meredith met me at the shoreline and helped me off the water. We took my boat back to the trailer, and Meredith checked the stroke coach, a device that calculates the rower's SPM. She asked if I knew my stroke rate. I had not looked at it once during the race. In my effort to race my mind had taken a holiday. I was just rowing and not thinking. Meredith said I had done 30-31 SPM for most of the race and had reached 32-33 for part of it. So I guess I was rowing fast but had no power. Super.

After the boat was back on the trailer I slumped in my chair, put on my Ipod, and tried not to act the way I felt: embarrassed, dejected, overwhelmed. Why did I ever pick this sport? I could be at home working in the yard or watching a golf tournament. I could be swimming or fishing with the kids. I ate a little, drank some Gatorade, and slowly got over my piss-poor performance. Ed soon showed up for our doubles race. Whether someone had pulled him aside and let him know about my race or he is just a decent human, I will never know. He did not ask me once about my singles race. If he had, I would have told him that I suck, and he should not row with me. But he never asked. We soon began rigging the double in preparation for the race.

When it was time, we took the boat to the water, put the oars on the boat and got in. Ed told me as we launched what we should do for a warm-up. We would start out slow and then do a series a ten fast and ten slow until we reached about three hundred yards past the start. We would then do a couple of starts for good measure. We went through the routine, and my nerves settled. It was time to get in line for the race.

I was an old hand at this now. We slotted in by asking people what race they were in until we found our group. We slowly rowed to the start. The starter soon called our race. This time there were five boats. We each rowed to our lane. A little jockeying of the rowers by the starter, and we were off. This time we were not the last off the line. We actually had a reasonable start. Not the fastest but at least we were not embarrassing. For the first seven hundred yards we made a race of it. There were three boats with us, all working hard. About one hundred and fifty yards from the finish, I began to feel an exhaustion that I had never felt. Ed must have felt me lose some power. He yelled that we only had about thirty more seconds to row. I tried to kick it up a notch but was overwhelmed by exhaustion.

We finished last. Unfortunately for Ed, he was rowing with an aerobic midget with poor rowing skills. I had never felt such exhaustion. My lungs felt like raisins. I cursed every single cigarette I had ever smoked in my younger years. I had given everything and come in last. I apologized to Ed and promised to work harder.

As we rowed to shore, the lactate cough kicked in. This happens because during a race lactic acid builds in your body. If you work hard enough for a long enough time, the lactic acid levels in your body will accumulate to the point that your body does things, like force you to cough, to try to clear it. When you get the cough, you know you have worked your tail off. I reasoned that I had worked hard and still come in last. So my fitness must still not be good enough. My rowing technique needed some serious fine tuning too.

We had one more race that day. I was in a quad (four rowers) for a race that afternoon. Ed and I were to join two other rowers. I cannot say I was really looking forward to the race at this point. After two last-place finishes, the thought of being fodder for another's rowing glory was less than appetizing. But I hung out, trying vainly to act interested and excited for the race. As we carried the boat to the water I suddenly realized that the four of us had never rowed as a group. This should be interesting. I would be in the three seat for the race and would have to follow the lead of the stroke, or four seat. I had never rowed with this person and was completely unfamiliar with his stroke. As a group we had never practiced starts. I was anticipating another stellar finish to my already stellar day.

We got loaded, pushed off, and spent about 2000 meters getting used to each other. We started out slow, did ten fast strokes, then ten slow a few times, and practiced two starts. This was the extent of our prep. It was what is was. Time to shut up and row.

We paddled over to the race lineup and advanced to the starting line. Given that this was my third race of the day, and my nerves had settled a bit, I took some time to look around on our way to the starting line. It was a beautiful day and the river was pretty. Rowers from other boats and other teams were wishing us luck (maybe we looked like we needed it). Even my inner cynic was soothed. We lined up and waited for the starter.

Ready
Attention
Row

We were off with a decent start. We did our thing. While I am sure I looked a bit like a downed helicopter's blades slapping the water, we were actually doing okay, which I defined as not being last. I could actually see a boat behind us, and we were head to head with another boat. As we pulled our last few strokes into the finish, I was surprised to see that we had not finished last. Next to last, but not last. The other rowers were probably carrying me. (There are rowers who call a quad with a weak rower "a three plus," and I was probably the plus.)

It had been a long day, and I was beat. We rowed back to shore, spilled out of the boat in a middle-aged, ungainly way. We got organized to take the boat back to the trailer. It was the march of complete defeat for me. I had two last-place and one next-to-last-place finishes. It was definitely my Dunkirk. After a slug or two of Gatorade, we began the derigging process again to load the boats back on the trailer for the trip home.

Meredith and I gathered our stuff and made the trek back to our car. At one point during the trip home, I heard some clinking going on next to me. I looked over and saw Meredith with a number of medals in her hand. Since you only get medals for first place, it means she had won in all three of her races. A nice finish to my day. My Dunkirk, her VE day. Here I am about to keel over from lack of oxygen, and she is shining medals to add to her collection. While I was proud of her accomplishment, the vast canyon between our results was an ego killer.

Rather than spend time on my miserable performance, we talked about her races. I learned in which race she was behind and had to work to catch up, which she led post to post, and which races she felt good or bad about. While I am sure she knew my results, she was nice enough not to bring it up in any meaningful way. But she did remind me about all the losses she had accumulated at various races and that getting competitive is about a four-year process.

First, you have to get in shape to compete, then you have to learn to race, and then you have to learn to win. Marlene had also told me that the getting in shape is a three- to four- year process. I licked my wounds in silence, drove home, and helped unload the car. After all this, I headed into the house to the place where the Jack Daniels was buried. I poured as big a drink as I thought I could without inspiring wifely disapproval. I made a similar but smaller drink for Meredith. We sat outside and watched the kids playing in the backyard with the dogs. It was the best part of the day.

12

The Winds were Changing

Recall that I had hatched a plan to quickly be good enough to be a problem to my wife, Meredith. I soon realized that the effort to get to an intermediate level was going to take a while. Just the aerobic fitness requirements to compete in this sport are stringent, especially when, like me, you start at a zero aerobic base.

But my attitude toward the sport was slowly changing. When people asked innocently if I enjoyed rowing, I was ready with a cynical answer: enjoyment is not something I would attribute to a sport with this much aerobic work. Despite my cynical attitude, I was actually learning to like rowing.

There was a rhythm to the workouts. You did some low-cardio at a low level, some power, some low-cardio at a higher level, some threshold and a little above threshold work. If you did this and add some weights and maybe some off-the-water low-cardio work in order to use some different muscles, you became fitter. You could measure your progress with lactic acid tests and erg races.

There was also the competition. While there are plenty of rowers who enjoy going out and rowing for rowing's sake, I cannot say that I had met many of them. Maybe it was that the club where I belong is full of type-A weirdos in constant need of ego gratification that an occasional win provides them. But it does not seem like it.

Most masters rowers just seem to like the sport. The competition seems to be a way to measure their fitness and quality of rowing against others. Not every master rower is an aerobic giant either. People seem to commit at different levels. Some train hard and want badly to win; others merely compete and are happy if they do not finish last.

After my first race I realized that my goals were changing. I still wanted to be a pain in the rear to my rowing wife. After all, this is the same woman who challenged me to a forty-yard dash on our second date. She had been a track athlete in her younger days, running the 400 and 800. Meredith had maintained her athletic shape better than I had. So the challenge arose. While I would tell you who won, it would be ungentlemanly of me to gloat. So you will have to ask her who won.

I wanted to be good enough to be competitive with Meredith, but I was also enjoying the work for the work's sake. The challenge was much greater than I had anticipated. The challenge and the competition had sucked me in. Judging by my first race, I was definitely not competitive, and realizing that led to a round of PRD (post-race depression). But it also made me want to work harder. I was challenged by the fact that rowers of all sizes and skills could move the boat better than me.

After the race I asked the coaches what I needed to do. They talked about the improvements I needed to make in my stroke. They said that my aerobic fitness would come and that it was clear that I did not have any issues with the amount of work I was doing. I asked our head coach what were the two or three things I most needed to improve. He handed me a Post-it note with five things, not two or three. Swell. Every time I rowed I focused on one of them. I am not sure I improved much because I still get yelled at about all five. But I worked on them. One day I might do catch drills. Another day, release drills. Another day I would work on the pivot. Then I might work on my slide control. I did all this within the workout framework, which meant that the warm-up and cool-down times were used for drills.

We also had a new coach. Her name was Anya. Her reputation was that she had been a lightweight on the Russian National Team. I asked her to give me private lesson one day after hearing Meredith extol her virtues. So I took my single down to the water and climbed in for my lesson. She met me on the water in her launch and gestured for me to row.

Her English was poor, so I expected demonstrations of what she wanted me to do. After a few minutes of warming up, I heard a Russian accented "stop, stop, stop." When I looked up, Anya was shaking her head buried in her hands. Was something in her eye? Yep..my less-than-impressive rowing. She was covering her face avoid seeing this rowing abomination.

She slowly came to and made a motion like she was going to the catch. She made the motion of what she saw in my catch, then she motioned what she wanted it to look like. Okay, there is a difference? I must have looked like I did not understand. She did an exaggerated version of my catch, then her desired catch. Anya had this habit of making a goofy face when demonstrating my form while making a serene happy face when demonstrating the correct form. Do I actually make that face when I am rowing, or is she just mocking the quality of my skills? So it went for the entire lesson. Much head shaking and demonstration.

I worked on the things I was learning and hoped that it would make a difference. I knew from my golf days that to get better, sometimes you had to deconstruct what you were doing and reassemble it all over again. And surprisingly I wanted to. I wanted to get better. I did not care anymore about what the doctor had said. Fitness was a nice subtext for what I was doing, but I was now just enjoying the rowing and the training.

I was Rowing Man. Finishing last did not feel good, but I realized it was part of the process. I could complain and be embarrassed. I would join the comments of other rowers and complain about what the coaches were teaching us. After all, we are Americans, and we have a right to bitch. It is in the Constitution. But you had to go through the process to get better.

I also began to notice the commitment that others gave to the sport. Many members of our club had started as a result of their children's rowing career. What would cause the parent of a rowing child to start this sport? Is watching their children's aerobic pain and long hours of practice not enough? Do parents of javelin throwers get a sudden urge to chuck a spear over and over? I do not get it. Yet, probably a quarter of our club members started as a result of their children's involvement. There are two families in particular that were good examples.

One family had three sons who rowed in high school. One went on to row at Cornell University and the other two at the University of Wisconsin. One of the sons was part of the boat that won the 2008 Intercollegiate Rowing Association Championship Regatta. So not only were the three sons rowing forces of nature but so are the parents. The wife was a very accomplished tennis player and completely quit to sit on her bohunkas and go backwards. She became one of the better masters rowers. The husband was the one who beat me during the January ergathon. My story was that he must have cheated. But he was clearly committed to getting better.

Another family was similar. Their son was a high school rower who rowed at Trinity in Hartford, one of the good Division 3 schools. After he graduated, he went on to the national team and was working to be part of the lightweight squad. Both the husband and wife started rowing soon after their son started in the sport. Both come to the club almost every day to row, sweat, and go to regattas.

How does this happen? Wouldn't golf and running combo be more fun and just as aerobically satisfying? I am not sure I get it, but it happens. It was happening for me. At first I thought it was a reaction to having to get back in shape. But I was realizing that the sport was becoming part of my life. I was reading *Rowing News* and looking forward to getting it once a month. I was starting to know the competitive college teams. I wanted to see how certain masters rowers did in certain regattas. I was watching the progress of the national team as they prepared for the Olympics.

What was happening to me?

Here I was with a bunch of Yankees doing an aerobic sport and enjoying it. I guess that finishing last was so much fun that I just had to have more.

13

Black Hawk Down

After Derby, the next regatta I planned to compete in was three weeks away in Princeton, New Jersey, on Lake Carnegie. After a couple days of rest and a few handfuls of Advil to relieve the aches and pains, I returned to my training. Ed and I talked about going to this race, but Ed passed on the three-hour drive to Princeton. We continued to train together several times a week in the double, and I continued to work in the single on the five things in which I needed to improve. Occasionally I was placed in this or that boat by the coaches to fill a boat in need of a rower.

I knew I had to improve certain parts of my stroke. Despite my efforts to work on the five parts of the stroke the coach suggested, I was still receiving a stream-of-conscience coaching with every row. Everyday seemed to be my day to have the coaches over concentrate on my poor rowing style. Finish the stroke, elbows up, cleaner finishes, more compression, relax at the catch, accelerate your arms not your slide at the catch, pivot before the slide, and get the right ratio—these seemed to be coaching favorites for me. One piece of advice to rowing coaches: focus on one or two things each day for the rower to work on. It is hard to work on ten pointers all at once!

As the regatta approached, the coaches said I would be doing a double with Ken and my single again. With the line ups set, I approached Ken and suggested we row several times to get used to each other. We set a schedule and did several workouts together. We did some slow rows, some threshold, and some power pieces. We worked on starts. We were ready, or as ready as we could be with me in the boat.

On the day of the race, Meredith and I loaded the car as before. But this time we were cartopping our singles. Although I had seen boats cartopped, I never appreciated the awkwardness of driving with a twenty-seven-foot boat on top of the car. If you are unfortunate enough to stop too far into an intersection, a truck coming through that intersection could be wearing the front end of your boat. No wonder the state of Pennsylvania outlaws it. We were also meeting several other rowers to car pool on the way to Princeton. Do not own a Suburban if you do not want other rowers to ride with you. We hit the road at around six a.m., loaded and ready.

Given our fully loaded situation, there thankfully were no incidents on the way to the regatta. We drove through Princeton and got to the site on the lake where the competitors congregate. There was not much parking space, and cars were being directed to side streets. Since we had boats on top of the car, we were allowed to get into a small parking lot to unload. We were then to move the car to the side street for parking. After the car was unloaded, I "forgot" to move it, but no one seemed too out of sorts with its presence. I was not looking forward to reparking and walking two miles back to the race venue. I am Rowing Man, not walking man. A fine start to the day, I thought. Could this be a good omen?

We rigged boats and waited impatiently for our race. I was told to warm up about thirty minutes before we went on the water for our double race. So I did six rounds of twenty jumpies. Jumpies are the unmanly name for deep squats with a jump after the compression. After that exercise I was glad to have some rest before the race. The coaches told me that getting your lactic acid up and processing through it was good just before a race. My legs were hurting and tired. I hoped the coaches were right.

Finally, it was time for me and Ken to make the trek to the dock. We grabbed the boat and some other club members grabbed oars, and we marched. We put the boat into the water, put the oars in their oarlocks and rowed off the dock. I was feeling better about this race. I had raced before and knew what to expect. I was an old hand. I was smiling to myself and thinking about what kind of warm-up we should do when we buried the boat into a sand bar. And not just a bump, but a full-blown bury.

We could not get off the sand bar. My thoughts of glory were replaced with thoughts of getting out of the boat to relieve us of our glued position. I was getting a sinking feeling, but it was not coming from the boat. We were beached. Thankfully, Ken was able to get a pretty good purchase of the sand with his oar and push us off the sand bar. Ken apologized, saying he was not really paying attention. Really? I would not have known if he had not said anything.

The shoaling of our boat sort of threw me off the warm-up I had been thinking about. We paddled silently to the line-up. (Maybe if we row slowly, will we get to the start after the other rowers are through laughing.) As we waited for the start, Ken asked if we were going to do anything different for the race. I thought we should just do it like we did in practice, but I added a little extra. I told him that our goal for this race was to not be DFL (dead blankety last). Ken cheerfully accepted the challenge.

When the race was called, we rowed to the start. When everyone was even, we were off. A decent start was followed by leveling off at 30-31 SPM. I was working hard. Meredith had told me that if you do not feel like crap after the first 250 meters, then you are not working hard enough. Well, I felt like crap. My brain was telling me to slow down. So I decided to start thinking about maintaining form to get my brain from focusing on the hurt. This lasted for a few minutes.

Ken suddenly yelled "300 meters to go." I hoped that was my signal to pour it on. I picked up the SPM a couple of strokes. I counted every stroke, trying to keep my mind focused on something other than the intense work. The horn sounded when I had counted to about 36, signaling that we had crossed the finish.

I was so tired I could not row another stroke. I slumped in the boat, clumsily grabbed for the water bottle, took a drink and poured some over my head. After thirty seconds we started paddling back to the dock. I had no clue how we had finished. I didn't think we were last, but handicaps can kill you. Master rowers get time handicaps for their age. The older the rower, the more time handicap you receive. I thought that most of us in the race were about the same age, so I was hopeful that we had not been handicapped to a last place finish.

We got to the dock and unloaded with as much grace as I could muster. We pulled the boat out of the water and brought it back to the trailer. After a few minutes of time in the club revival tent, drinking fluids and eating a banana, the final times were posted for the race. Ken and I wandered down to the board and looked. It was official. We were not DFL. We were next to DFL. Success!

I had some time before my next race. I tried to relax, wandering the regatta grounds and picking up some food at the food tent. I didn't want to eat too much, but I worried about having some fuel in the tank for my next race. Soon enough it was time to go. Meredith helped me with the single, picking up the bow while I carried the stern in one hand and my sculls (oars) in the other. As we put the boat in the water, I noticed that my foot stretcher was loose. So while I worked the screws to tighten the foot stretcher, Meredith placed the oars in the oarlocks and tightened them down. I got in the boat and pushed off the dock.

I cannot convey the lonely feeling of a single. While not quite Hemingway-esque, it is just you and two oars on about twelve inches of width and three to four inches of height separating you from the deep blue. I did a semi-warm-up on the way to the start line up. I made sure I avoided the sand bar. It would not have been good to bury two boats. Of course, my avoidance only supports our coach's argument that masters rowers do not take care of club boats like the double that got stuck on the sand bar. We had scratched the bottom badly, and the boat would need repainting. The coaches would argue that with my boat, I was more careful.

Having avoided the sand bar, all systems were go. I actually felt more confident than I expected. I got into the race lineup more hopeful, until I saw the competition. One guy was probably thirty-five years old and had no body fat—I mean none—and a shaved head. Another rower was six-foot-six and looked to be my age, only like an NFL tight end who had slimmed down. The other rower was the guy Meredith identified as a great rower who wins a lot of races. I could not see the fourth rower, thankfully.

We got in the lineup, and I did the creep to the start again. I did not want to back row. When we were in line, the start cadence began and we were off. I did a half, half , three-quarter, and began to lengthen. I settled to a 31 SPM and was pulling well. I could only see the sterns of the other boats. So they were ahead of me. I doubled down on my effort, and then I flipped. I bit the dust, I went for a snorkel, or whatever term rowers use. As my head came out of the water and I cleared my eyes, I noticed that my oar had come out of the oarlock. The same oars that Meredith had been so nice to put in for me. This means that the oarlock had not been closed and screwed down correctly. Instead, I was completely screwed.

One of the chase boats came over to check if I was okay. They watched as I attempted in vain to get back in the boat. Getting back into one of these skinny boats from a drenched position is akin to trying to change sitting positions atop a flag pole. I tried a couple of times to crawl back in without success. The chase boat pilot bailed me out. He grabbed the boat, put it cross wise on the back of his launch, scooped me out of the water and brought me back to the dock.

Embarrassed, I told the chase boat pilot that an oar popped out of the oarlock. See, mister, it's not my fault; it was an equipment failure. Normally, I would not have flipped. He said he had seen the splash down and asked how long I had been rowing? Did my beautiful style give me away? I wondered. Was it my slow start? Or was it the Goodyear tire I carry with me at all times? I replied that I had started the previous fall. He smiled and said, "it gets better." No compliments. No comments on how quickly I was racing a single. Just "it gets better." Man, I must look like crud out there.

Several members of the club were there to meet me at the dock. And, as always, your friends seem to have the most fun with your ignominy.

Scott, you look wet
I give a ten for the degree of difficulty on that flip
Is the water warm?
Nice day for a swim

Meredith was there to meet me too. She asked what had happened. I told her that an oarlock had flipped open and gave her the look. One of the club members on the dock asked her if it was, in fact, she who had put in the oars. She looked up, smiled and said, "Got to keep the man down."

Now, here I am all wet due to an equipment malfunction that could arguably be laid at her feet, and she comes up with one of the best lines of her entire life. It was tough not to smile. Of course, there were huge guffaws from my supposed rowing friends.

Undoubtedly, I learned an important rowing lesson: the rower is ultimately responsible for checking the gear to make sure it is right. I had not done that. I figured Meredith knew what she was doing. But in her defense, and as hard as it is to say, every boat is different. Since the rower is most familiar with the boat, it is the rower's responsibility for the equipment. A lesson I learned with a swim.

I learned another important lesson that day as well. Spandex drying on your body just ain't that comfortable. A bit itchy, a bit tight, and now a bit rank. A combo of race wetness and lake wetness would not endear me to my travel compatriots. I had to remember to bring a change of clothes when packing for regattas. Despite the loaded car, I might just be able to squeeze it in.

We soon packed up for the trek home. As we drove I tallied the results of my racing career. Two groundings, two last-place finishes, two next-to-last-place finishes, and a flip. Too bad I am a bit old. Otherwise, the Olympic team would be calling. After all, we were right there in Princeton, where they train. I wonder if the Olympic coaches saw my spectacular flip. I did meet one of the Olympians from the men's eight. Our coach had trained him in high school. He was about six feet four inches and weighed about 220 pounds. I overheard him telling someone that he was down to 6 percent body fat. Maybe the Olympic team will not be calling me.

There were some offsets to the spectacular race results, though. I had lost about fifteen pounds since I started rowing. So much for my "it's just water weight" argument. I had recently gone to the pulmonologist to check on my asthma and had learned that my lung function was the best it had been in years. Also my blood pressure was down ten points on both the diastolic and systolic readings. All good things that were driven by trying to compete in a sport that is viewed by many as a sport that is in the top three for fitness requirements.

All these good things were accruing without any single injuries to my fifty-four-year-old body. Sure, there were aches and pains but nothing serious. Knock on wood. When I had gone through my jogging phase in my late twenties, I was constantly nursing some injury. I was now working with a number of committed athletes. These were people who took the sport seriously but still had fun with it. Despite my less-than-stellar showing, I was enjoying it. I had to keep reminding myself that this is a four-year process and bad results were just the beginning of the learning and training.

14

Rowing Camp Re-Redux

July and most of August came and went. I was still training with Ed a few days a week and doing my single. While I could not row all I wanted due to travel and other commitments, I was rowing enough. I hoped I was getting better. But you never really know until there are races.

Meredith went to more races than I did. I figured why push it in my first year? I needed the training as much or more than I needed the racing. I knew that I was not in the shape to compete with better rowers. Also Head race season was coming. These were 4000 to 5000 meter races that lasted about twenty minutes (or more probably for the weak ones like myself). I needed to kick up the length of my threshold work to get faster for these races. In the interim, Meredith had scheduled us to go the Craftsbury again for a long weekend in August. So one Friday in August we loaded up the car, said goodbye to the kids and Meredith's mother, and made the four-hour trek to northern Vermont.

I knew what to expect this time and was prepared with lots of OTC pain relievers. Craftsbury usually rotated the coaches in the summer months. I was met by a new set this time. Meredith had seen a few of them before on her various trips there, but they were new faces to me. Not that it mattered much. I would love to be trained by the top coaches in the country. But given my level of inexpertise, would it really matter? A national team coach would have probably just rolled their eyes at the sight of my rowing. A national team coach would say, Scott…have you thought about bowling? Better just to know that the coaches were good, dedicated folks and move on.

We started that afternoon getting filmed during our row. I took out a single and rowed down the lake waiting for the launch with the film crew. When they got to me, I tried to display my best rowing form. Sit up, do not slouch. Nice compression at the catch and a strong finish. As much as I was saying this to myself, I was not producing it on the water. I was all over the place. My balance just did not seem to be there. I was rocking at the catch and getting my oars too deep throughout the stroke. I would be interested to hear what the coaches were going to tell me at the film review that night. I would be interested to know if the coaches were sniggering up their sleeves at my prowess when they looked at the video before the rowers entered the room.

We rowed around the lake a few times, got a few pointers, and went in. We got cleaned up for dinner. I went to the store and bought a six pack of beer, which we put a dent in before dinner. Dinner was the usual healthy fare in which Craftsbury specializes. After dinner, we went for the video review. I got more out the review this time than the previous time. I could actually see the strengths and weaknesses of other's rowing. When my turn arrived it was obvious what my problem was. I was rowing over the barrel badly. This means that after I put my blades in at the catch, I was pulling up and was not parallel with the gunnel of the boat. This was causing me to unset the boat and screw up my finish. One of the coaches pulled me aside later and said that we would be working on drills the next day to correct this problem.

At the dock the next morning the coaches broke us into groups and told us where to meet on the lake. We all piled into our boats and rowed to our spots. I was with the group that would focus on blade work.

Our first drill was called the turtle drill. I realize now that there is a theme developing in my rowing career. I have no clue why things are called what they are called. Why is this drill called the turtle drill? I have no clue. I do not ask. I just accept it and move on. I must be the least curious person on earth. And yes, I like to navigate without a map and do not like asking for directions. Anywho, in this drill you go to the catch, put your blades in the water, and keep the same body position you had at the catch throughout the whole stroke. The idea is to teach correct blade depth. Since you do not swing the body but only use your legs and arms on the stroke, it is impossible to bury your blades. We did this several times, and it worked. The boat all of a sudden felt lighter and moved better. When I went back to a normal stroke I was amazed at how much better the boat felt. The finish also seemed more clean.

The next drill I worked on a release drill. One of the coaches said I was working too hard at the finish to feather my blades. When I pushed down to get the oars out of the water, he wanted me to just open my hands a little, and let the water feather the blades for me. This sounded a bit suspicious, but I tried it. After a few minutes of practice, it actually worked. No more trying to pry the knife out of moving butter. I went the whole length of the lake doing this.

When I got to the end of the lake, the coach told me to now just add a slight flick with the thumb and forefinger, and I would have a decent finish. So I tried this. Amazing. After all this time of trying to figure out the finish, this was all it took. No more big overemphasized movement. No huge rotation of the wrists to try and pry the oars out. This was pretty simple and easy. I spent the rest of the day actually enjoying myself. The boat felt lighter and moved better. It seemed I was a bit faster than before.

At the end of the day, we put our boats away, stretched, showered, finished the beer, and headed for dinner. I actually enjoyed dinner that night given my newfound rowing talent. Chicken, some veggie potpourri, polenta, salad, and some whole grain rolls never tasted so good. I am sure I was overly chatty, animated and completely out of character. But I felt good about what had happened today and was looking forward to tomorrow.

The next day we spent the morning working on our new-found rowing techniques. We both received a few tips here and there. During the morning row one of the coaches came over and said my blade depth and set of the boat were much better. He told me to pick up the boat to a 30 SPM. I did, and for the first time the boat did not feel like I was rowing two of me. It was awesome. Maybe I might not be the king of DFL anymore. Our next race was a few weeks away at Mystic, Connecticut, and I could not wait.

15

Magical Mystic Tour

Ed and I had decided to row the Coastweeks Regatta in Mystic, Connecticut. This is small regatta sort of kicks off head-race season. While it is not really a head race, as the course is not much over 2000 meters, it is a good warm-up for the soon to come 4000 to 5000 meter races. Ed and I were to do the double, and the coaches put us in a quad. On the morning of the race Meredith and I did the usual load and go. After my wet Princeton experience, I made sure I had a change of clothes.

We got there about nine a.m. We were not in a hurry, since our races were a little later that day. It was September but unusually cold and wet. Highs were in the low sixties and there was a cold mist all day. Great weather for a duck, but there was no lightning, and the race went off without a hitch. Ed and I got together about an hour before our race and rigged the boat. We brought the boat down to the water shortly after the rigging was finished and proceeded to row to the start. Finally, we could get in a longer warm-up; it was a full race distance to the start. We went through our warm-up twice. Given the cold and wet, a long warm-up was especially nice, as I was feeling a bit like a wet dog.

The start of our race was finally announced. As opposed to a sprint race, the boats do not start together. The starter calls boats by their bow number, a number placed in a holder on the bow of the boat. When you pass the starting line and break the timer, you start the race. I considered this a positive for team Ed and Scott. I would not be embarrassing the team with my splashy effort to make the boat move from a dead stop.

When our bow number was called, we did a few hard strokes, got the speed up and plowed through the start. We were on our way. I was excited to use the newfound rowing techniques I had acquired at rowing camp. Ed and I had practiced doing 28-30 SPM and being able to do it for longer periods of time. After beginning the race at 30 SPM rate we settled to 27. Given the shortness of the race, this was probably a mistake. The good rowers were pulling closer to 30. But ignorance is bliss. The race seemed like a pretty long way to me. A race of over a mile lasting somewhere around nine to ten minutes seemed like an immense challenge. So I was hesitant to go out too hard.

We were rowing well. The race was feeling easy. I was thinking that all my training was finally kicking in. This is what racing should feel like when you are in condition. Then I remembered the first maxim of rowing: if you feel good, you are not rowing fast enough. What a boneheaded move. I had gone out as if this was just one of our training pieces. I yelled back to Ed that I was picking it up. At about that time I noticed that the boat behind us was starting to close the distance. Since the boats were starting with about a twenty-second cushion between them, the boat behind us had probably closed the gap by twelve seconds or so. Ed and I began to pour it on. Not that anyone could notice, but it felt harder. I was rowing with sweat coming out of every part of me, but I am not that sure that my increased stroke rate was moving the boat any faster. I sort had the impression that I was working harder without much effect on the boat.

The boat behind was slowly gaining on us. Somehow we were able to keep them about twenty to thirty yards off our stern at the finish. But once again, I was finished at the finish. I slumped in my seat trying to regain my breath, while Ed tried to get me to paddle off the course and get out of the way of other finishers. I must have been really out of it because I do not remember even rowing to help Ed move the boat away from the finish. When I regained some semblance of normal brain function, we paddled our way back to the dock. We unloaded, picked the boat up and brought it back to a set of slings so other rowers could readjust the boat for their race.

Our coach came over soon and asked how the race went. I unloaded my tale of woe. Even with my disappointment, the coach said we did a good job fighting off the other boat. I almost fell over. A compliment? What was that? Soon the times were posted, and we had finished seventh out of fifteen boats. Again, I almost fell over. The trip to Craftsbury had made all the difference, and it was so simple. All I had needed to do was solve the blade depth problem. I was now excited for me and Ed to tackle the quad race. This should be interesting.

Our quad was loaded with three good rowers and me. Another three-plus. We had only rowed together once, and the stern rower, a former collegiate rower, was kind to point out a few problems of mine he was feeling from his seat. The stern can feel what is going on in the boat by watching the water and feeling the effect on his slide by the other rowers. I was the most inexperienced rower in the boat. If there were issues with how the boat was moving, chances are that I was doing it. It is nice living with a target on your back for any bad rowing efforts.

Soon it was time to load for the quad race. We grabbed the boat and walked it to the dock. We loaded our middle-aged cans (does fifty-four still qualify for middle aged, or am I now officially old?) into the boat and started the row to the starting line. We went through our warm-up. Since we had only rowed together once before, we tried a couple of starts. All felt okay so we hung out near the start until our race was called. We were excited when we realized that another men's quad from our club was starting right before us. The other quad from our club was a group of men who had rowed many races together and had won a fair number. Given their history, I was excited to race against them, but I was sure it would take a Herculean effort to beat them. Actually, one of the other members of our boat asked Ed, the bow, to keep an eye on them. He wanted Ed to yell if he thought we were falling behind.

When the first club quad was called, we got into the lineup and waited for our start call. I was invigorated; a good showing in the double will do that to you. We received our start call, and we were off. I was focused on not screwing up with more experienced rowers. I don't think I ever took my eyes off the back of the rower in front of me. I tried to stay in good rhythm, get my oars in at the same time as he did, and pull like a machine. I started hurting pretty bad about halfway through the race, so I assumed I was working hard enough. I don't think Ed paid any attention to the boat ahead of us; I heard no calls from him to force us to work harder to close the gap. The boat felt as though it was moving well. It had that light feel.

We got to the finish, and I was bushed. Two races fairly close together put the hurt on me. My legs were feeling the effects of a ton of lactic acid being pumped through them. After the on-water post-race rest we rowed back to the dock. My legs were so rubbery that I could not even take a full stroke.

When we returned to the dock, the coaches were smiling. I was not used to having the coaches pay me any post-race attention. But there they were, smiling and asking if we needed help. As we got out of the boat, one coach pulled me aside and said she thought we had beaten the other quad from our club. She said we had a better ratio and were moving the boat better as we approached the finish line. I was in shock. After less than a year of rowing, could I really compete at this level? Had my conditioning improved so much that I could go from zero to hero in just a few months?

When the results were posted, we had a faster water time than our other club boat by a few tenths. But we were handicapped to third place due to our younger age. No matter. It still felt great to be competitive. I was on cloud nine and was anticipating a great fall season. The Head of the Housatonic was just a few weeks away. A few weeks of training with Ed, and we would be ready with the newly found head of steam that we would be bringing to the competition. Let the trash talk begin. Better go buy some even tighter spandex to reduce wind resistance.

Even better, we received medals for our third-place finish. Most regattas only reward first-place finishers, so this was somewhat unexpected. It is a small thing, but I was proud of the ribbon hanging out of my coat. I had worked hard and been rewarded. I am now elite, a medal winner. As our medals were awarded, the official photographer asked us to smile for the camera. Now this is living.

The coaches could whack me around for a month. Other rowers could bark at me about my rowing style. Meredith could give me a full list of honey do's. Now all would be okay.

16

Need For Speed

After a day or two of rest, the work for the Head of the Housatonic began. The coaches knew Ed and I were most comfortable at a 26-stroke rate. They were pushing us to increase to 28. I tried to tell them that we were doing a 28-29 for most of our sprint races and that I was completely washed out after each of those four-minute races. But they were insistent. This meant not just getting there and rowing a 28 for a few minutes. It meant that we had to be able to race at that stroke rate for around twenty minutes, which seemed like an impossible task.

As usual I went to my source, rowing wife, to ask what stroke rate that she was using at head races. Meredith replied 28-30, which was not the answer I was looking for. Okay, so Ed and I had to figure it out. The next time we were to row, we talked it over. He suggested we do our next threshold pieces at this stroke rate but not use as much power. This seemed logical, but questions began floating up from deep within my rowing brain. If we are not pulling as hard, we will not be moving the boat as fast. Does that mean that the ratio (the time of the stroke versus the timing of the recovery) will be screwed up? Does this imply that we will be working fast but not moving the boat due to the poor ratio? Does this mean that more power and slower stroke rates are no longer the goal? So many questions and so little time. Did I consult the coaches with my questions? Nope.

Ed and I just went out and did the 28 SPM like we were told. The boat felt okay but not as good as when we rowed a 26. Since there was only so much time before the race, we were only able to practice a few more times. Despite the practice, 28 SPM for long periods felt forced and rushed. I was less than confident for the race but knew the coaches would be watching to make sure we rowed a 28. We practiced a few more times, and the fateful day arrived quickly.

On the day of the race, we arrived at the regatta around eight a.m. and took our stuff to the club trailer and met our team members. We unfolded our chairs, found a shady spot and sat down waiting for our races. The venue was filling up. This was going to be a huge race. High schools and clubs from all over were here to compete. As I sat wide-eyed staring at the goings on, another member informed me that many good rowers use this race as a tune up for the Head of the Charles.

The Head of the Charles is considered the most important race of the year. I do not know the historical reason for this, but as a new rower it is difficult to understand. Perhaps it is that you cannot just go and row if you pay the race fees. In the Head of the Charles you apply to enter. There are rumors, legends, and myths about the ways to get in. Legend has it that it is easy to get in the first time. From then on, a solid race performance with a time within 5 percent of the winning time in your division seems to guarantee a return. Otherwise, all bets are off. Does winning a lot of races during the season leading up to the Head of the Charles matter? Probably does not hurt, but no one seems to know for sure. Is there a lottery system to select rowers? That is the system described on the website, but no one seems willing to bet on it. There is one line on the website discussing the lottery process that drives everyone nuts: "Except for variances, which may only be granted by the Managing Directors." So what are the parameters around these variances? Why would one be granted and when? I dunno.

The big regattas like the Housatonic still surprise me a bit. Vendors of rowing paraphernalia line up in tents to sell all kinds of goodies boat makers, timing equipment, boat-transport equipment, and clothing. Rowers tend to be a fairly conservative lot clothing wise. They would never be confused with the golf crowd. Probably the brightest thing you see on the water during an average month is neon jackets or shirts, and that is so you do not get killed by the bigger, motorized boats. But you can find all sorts of flowery, plaid, and other sorts of bright rowing clothing for sale at regattas.

I also was beginning to notice a theme developing at regattas. Invariably, some number of rowers would show up in a fifteen-year-old car. Volvos were a favorite. On top of that fine piece of autocraft would be an equally old boat of some vintage or another, strapped to a homemade cartop carrier. Typically, the person getting out of the car would have a bandana tied to their noggins, a tie-dyed tee shirt on over their rowing togs, and Birkenstocks or clogs slapping around their feet. These folks would rig their boats in silence, bring them to the water and then be off for their race. Just as invariably, a first-, second-, or third-place finish would be their reward. And as silently as they arrived at the race, they would derig, slip their boats back on their cars, and leave. Who are these silent rowing ninjas who look like 1970s throwbacks?

As I waited and watched the race venue fill, I was fairly confident about the race Ed and I were in. We had done better at

Mystic. We had raced against a good quad from our club and had been found worthy. We had practiced at a higher stroke rate, and our form was improving. I had been to three rowing camps and learned an incredible amount. I didn't even think that perhaps the competition would be stronger here. Nor did I worry that my conditioning was behind that of the better rowers. I didn't worry that after less than a year of rowing, my technical skill set was subpar. After all I had seventh- and third-place finishes. I am clearly a fast learner and a medal winner. I am a rowing force of nature.

With confidence, Ed and I brought our boat down to the water when it was time. We launched, did our warm-up on the way to the start, and got in line for our race. When the starter called us, we accelerated to the start and broke the start line to begin the timer. I settled into our new 28 stroke rate and began the twenty-minute race. I was confident and feeling strong and cocky.

The one bad thing about facing backwards is that you can see the competition gaining on you. The saying "never look back, they may be gaining on you" does not apply. You know immediately when you are slow and useless. It was not long before three boats blew right past us. Blowing right past someone is not something that happens often in rowing. It is not like you are piloting an Indy race car. You're not going much faster than seven or ten miles per hour. But let me assure you that we were passed easily by these other boats. We were the blue hairs out for a Sunday drive on the interstate jamming up all the traffic. I was suspicious of some hidden propeller on these faster boats.

How could this happen? We were good finishers at Mystic. It must be the stroke rate, I thought. I brought the stroke rate down a notch to 26. The boat seemed to be moving better after thirty seconds or so. I yelled to Ed to let me know if we were close to passing anyone ahead of us. Unfortunately, he never said a word.

We rowed and rowed, then we rowed some more. The problem with a twenty-minute race is that there are lots of things to grab your attention in that time span. It is not like a 100-meter run that is over quickly. For me the distraction was that it was fall in New England. At one point in the race, I saw all the pretty trees. This is really beautiful being on the river today, I thought. The hills lining the river were showing colors of orange, yellow and red. I was feeling aerobically like crap, but I was smelling the roses. So this is why I row. What a beautiful venue. We probably lost a minute to the competition due to my lack of focus.

After what seemed like an eternity, Ed yelled that we had 50 more strokes, or little under two minutes left. Thank you, God. Time to quit looking at the trees. I really poured it on. Not that there was much left, but I yelled to Ed that I was picking it up. We brought the boat slowly to 29 SPM. I was counting every stroke. My mind and body said no, but somehow we held it together for those 50 strokes. I counted to 50, then 51, 52, 53. Ed yelled for 50 more strokes.

I cannot completely explain my feelings when the call for 50 more strokes hit my ears. I can tell you that my thoughts for Ed were not that amicable. I was happy that I did not have anything sharp around; I might have committed ritualistic suicide. I think, maybe, an F bomb may have slipped the surly bonds of earth. But we had a race. If we were going to finish well, we had to finish. I had to reload the brain to get through another 50 strokes. Row hard, watch your form, count every stroke: 35,

40, 45, 50, 51, 52, 53. I was expecting the finish any moment. I really wanted to hear that horn signaling the end to my pain. Ed yelled 20 more.

Now this was misery. Was Ed just messing with me to get me to row harder for five minutes? Was he paying me back for the bad finishes we had produced? Or had he innocently miscalculated? It does not matter, I thought, 20 more and hard. I was hearing the horn for other rowers, so I knew we were close. I could hear Ed telling me to row hard. Oh, this is rich, I thought. Here I am 120 strokes into a 50-stroke call, and he is telling me to row hard. I still gave it all I had to assuage my leaf peeping guilt. We eventually got to the finish.

As always, I was seriously hurting. How do others row through the finish and not slump, gasping for air and water? After my prescribed recovery minute, we turned the boat around to head back to the launch point. We had a nice slow row back to the launch with plenty of time to get the gears reworking. Unfortunately, the lactic acid cough was starting. I seemed to be the only one I knew that got this. I did not hear any of the other rowers hacking away like me on the way back to the launch point. Am I that out of shape, or do I give a superhuman effort? I *am* that out of shape, I guessed. Soon enough we were out of the boat and back at the trailer, where we derigged the boat.

Ed was excited to see how we did. I did not share his enthusiasm. Maybe the lactic acid had made Ed forget how quickly the other boats had passed us. Maybe he saw things of which I was not aware, since I do not turn around in the boat. Only he does. Maybe the extra 70 strokes had cut an electrical circuit in my brain, and I was not aware of our amazing speed.

After the post-race work, we went to the board to check our times, which the race officials were just posting when we got there. I looked, hopefully, beginning at the top and working down. I did not stop until we got to seventeenth. How many were below us? Two. We were seventeenth out of nineteen. Not DFL, but close. We had rowed the race in a bit less than nineteen minutes. The best boats had rowed it in just above sixteen minutes. We were approximately fifteen to twenty seconds slower than the best boats for every 500 meters we rowed. No wonder we had been passed so easily. I was feeling bad. I did not worry about Ed's call at the end of the race. Instead, as we humbly dragged our cans back to our trailer, I asked Ed if he still wanted to row with a lard boy. Ed laughed and said it takes two to row a double. Yeah, I thought, he was rowing and I was riding .I decided to leave it at that.

Since Meredith was not racing that day in an effort to save herself for the Head of the Charles, we went back to the car and began the forty-minute drive home. I was beat and since she was driving, I went into commute sleep. We were soon back at home and Meredith was pouring the Jack Daniels for the post-race memory eraser.

17

Valhalla

Meredith and her doubles partner had entered the Head of the Charles River (HOCR) for the second time and had gotten in for the doubles race. In 2007 they had been eleventh. While they were satisfied with that result, they wanted to do even better in the 2008 race. This time of year, much conversation at home and the club was focused on HOCR.

Meredith and her partner made a few trips to row the Charles in preparation for the race. They spent time was studying the river maps to figure out the best lines for taking the various bridges and turns to save time on the course. They reviewed other competitors' race results and rowing histories. There was an amazing amount of prep and worry going on—worry about rigging, oar length, how fast to row the various segments of the race. E-mails and conversations were abundant.

The afternoon before the race, the two women nervously packed the car and drove to Boston with their double on the roof rack. I stayed home because the kids had various commitments to sports and friends. I cannot say I was unhappy about it. Dealing with all the traffic and people on the race venue to see a small snippet of Meredith racing would not be on my list for fun. Boston goes crazy for this race. It is estimated that about three hundred thousand people line the banks of the Charles River to watch this race.

But being the supportive husband that I am, I promised to watch the race on the internet feed. Also unbeknownst to Meredith, I had e-mailed a good number of our non-rowing friends and family to let them know that they could catch part of the race on the internet. I told them Meredith's bow number and about when I thought they would be passing the camera. If Meredith had been aware of my subversion, I would have been subjected to severe torture.

I received a call from a nervous Meredith, informing me that they had arrived and were going to dinner. I was imagining the conversation Meredith and her partner were having, planning strategy and talking about the difficult spots in the river. A year ago, I would have rolled my eyes at this. But now I was a rower, and I understood the focus, though I had never experienced it. My races were mental fogs. Survival rows. Mostly I was hoping to hang on and not finish last. Successful some of the time but not often. Maybe if I planned races, Googled the competition so I knew their abilities, and made sure all my rigging was spot on it would lead to high finishes. Nah!

But this is what competitive rowers do, I guess. They plan. Can you actually perform to plans, or is it merely a mental distraction to make you think you are doing all you can for a good finish? They certainly believed in the five Ps: Proper Planning Prevents Poor Performance. I was still in CATIP mode—Christ Almighty, This is Painful.

The next morning I imagined what was going on for them but was quick to focus back on what I had going on that day. Ed and I were meeting at the club early to get in some high-stroke rate threshold work to prepare for our next race. We wanted to row two 5Ks at a 28-29 stroke rate. This was a challenge for us.

I fed the dogs, said good bye to the sleeping teens, and took off at 6:30 for an early Saturday row. I met the other non-HOCR-worthy rowers at the club as we took boats out of storage for our less-than-triumphant rows. Since a number of the high school students and a few of the non-DFL masters were at HOCR, the coaches had gone to Boston with them. The usual coaching staff was, therefore, not on the water with us. When the coaches are not present on a Saturday, then few of the masters rowers want to do the usual 5k races scheduled for the day. I agree with this thought process. Hey, the cat is away. Let the mice play. My body can certainly use a break. I am old. I deserve it.

Unfortunately, Ed and I had work to do for a race in which we would like to finish closer to the top than to the bottom. If Ed had been smart, he would not have shown up and sentenced me to do it in my single. After all, I was the beginner. My fitness and rowing style were highly correlated to our rowing unsuccess. Make me do the work. But Ed is a good human and was more than willing to work to help me be better.

We did our usual warm-up in preparation for the two 5Ks we were to attempt. Then we went to the point in the river where the coaches usually start us. We slowed to a stop at that point, drank water, and did our preparation. We cleared the mind of negative brain waves and looked around to make sure we had a clear line for the start. All was good, excepting that negative brain wave thing. So we were off. We rowed a strong start and settled into our 28 SPM. Oh, yeah...this is rowing.

We made our way down the river passing our non-racing club members. We were working. As we rowed past other members, I was thinking they must certainly be impressed by our effort. No coaches were around, but we were doing the usual workout. What commitment we exhibit! We would be the envy of all. How dumb am I? Most would be wondering what the heck we were doing. We should be using the no coaching break for an easy row.

We rowed out to the harbor and were hit by the rollers that a southeastern wind always seems to bring. I had to slow to a 26 SPM to keep the boat moving in a good fashion. Ed tried to get me to pick it up, but the combination of the waves and my rough water inexperience dictated a 26. We were finally at the 5000-meter mark and stopped rowing to catch our breaths.

It had been painful. Not as painful as a real race but painful. We turned around and got set for the race back. After a ten-minute rest, we started the second race. The same wave issues hit us on the way back. For the first part of the race we were rowing 26 SPM. As we got further into the harbor we were able to pick up the stroke rate to 28. We ended up doing 28 for about 3000 meters. It was good. We had no clue if we were fast or slow as we had no other boats to compete with. Though we did not have any speed comparisons on this effort, our race mojo was on the rise. We rowed back to the dock after we were finished, confident in our abilities. Schuylkill, watch out. We will wake the other racers with our speed. Boo Yah!!!

We returned to the dock, washed and put away the boat and oars, and I ventured back home to face my hungry children. I am not sure what is worse—cleaning up their mess when they attempt to make breakfast or having to make the breakfast. In any event they always seem to opt for me to make it for them. After breakfast it was time to start the Saturday sports routine, running here and there, watching this and that and trying to pawn the trip back home on some other unsuspecting parent. I wanted to get back to see the part of Meredith's race on the internet. I was able to get back to the house around one fifteen. Since Meredith's race started some time close to 1:30, I would need to log onto the race coverage.

I grabbed a quick sandwich—do not want to be hungry while waiting for her double to go by—and logged onto the race website. I clicked on all the buttons to get the camera working and waited. At about two o'clock, I could see Meredith's boat in the distance. As she got closer, I could see that Meredith's boat was trying to pass another boat. Both were fighting for the good line through a bridge. It looked like there was little yelling between the boats for the line. Good stuff—pissed-off rowers yelling at each other. I am always amazed that anyone has the energy toward the end of a race to get into a verbal confrontation. I guess that is why interboat race confrontation is so uncommon. Usually by that point in a race I am trying to hang on to as much oxygen I can find. As the rowers got to the bridge the camera moved away from them and focused on the next set of rowers.

I had a few minutes to kill so I went back to the lineup sheet. I realized that Meredith was fighting for the line with a boat that had started ahead of theirs. So they had caught up. It was also a boat that had beat them in the prior year. By the time I had done all my fact checking, the final race results were being posted. Meredith's boat had come in seventh, up from eleventh the prior year. Thankfully, there would be no post-race depression.

Meredith's and her partner's performance always got me motivated. They win some and lose some, but they win more often than lose. I went downstairs for about thirty minutes and did some low-cardio work on the stationary spin bike. I realized this was a little obsessive, but I was pumped by their performance. Hard work pays off, so I will work hard. The little voice in my head said that this low-cardio work makes a difference. But as I sat there riding away, I thought about the fact that the bike was not moving. Yes, I know—that's why it's called a *stationary* bike. But could all this work without going anywhere be a metaphor for my rowing career. Will I be working my can off only to finish at the bottom of the pack forever?

This was getting a little too deep for me. We will leave these existential questions for the Harvard rowers. I am a Vandy guy, and we do not even have a rowing team. So I will work, sweat, and claim to be happy about my crappy finishes.

18

Flying to Close to the Sun

It was another week until my final race of the season. I had returned to training a few days after the last race. But I was frustrated. How could I dedicate so much time to something and still have so much more to do? I e-mailed Marlene to let her know that my last race was coming up. I would need to return to my winter training schedule soon. The fall weather would be turning bad, and we would not be able to go out on the water. She asked via e-mail how my season was going. Of course, I complained like the child I am. The good thing about having a coach that you communicate with via e-mail is that you can whine without the other person realizing what a complete wimp you are. You can put all kinds of words around your sad complaints and not sound like the six-year-old you truly are. How long is this going to take? How much more work must I do before I'm in reasonable shape for this sport? Does it take this long for everyone, or am I just that special?

Her reply was in her usual level-headed mode. She suggested that I not worry about it much. She reminded me in a nice way that my aerobic fitness was weak when we did my first set of training tests. Someday I think she is just going to say to me I was the worst physical specimen she ever tested, and it was going to take more than 180 days to get in strong enough shape. She also reminded me that I had been rowing for about a year. Yet

I was comparing myself to rowers who had years of experience. She asked how many years of experience the winning rowers at my club had.

Marlene was being way too logical. I was losing my angry thoughts. She suggested that shortly after my last head race, I should try a 2k erg test and see if I had gotten any better. Whether she did this to shut me up, I do not know. But the thought of doing a 2k race on the erg did not have much appeal. So I tucked my tail between my legs and continued training.

Ed and I continued to work on rowing comfortably at 28 SPM for longer periods. Our effort resulted in some improvement, but I would not say we had found rowing Valhalla. We struggled to hold it for twenty-minute threshold pieces. Our splits during these workouts were all over the place. But it was slowly getting better. I am sure that if Ed had a better rower with him, there would have been no struggle. Unfortunately for Ed, he had me to row and train with. Ed said he thought we were getting faster. I hoped he was right.

My oldest son, Logan, came to visit us during the time between the Housatonic and the Schuylkill races. He is another sports force of nature, like Meredith. He had played football and lacrosse in high school and had been co-captain of both teams. He had gone to college and turned himself into a D1 football player despite his five-foot-nine stature. He had lifted and run and gained weight until he was a 225-pound linebacker who made the 1,200-pound club (lifting 1,200 pounds of total weight by combining the weights lifted on one squat, one bench, and one clean).

He was always interested in this rowing obsession. He asked to see the kinds of workouts I was doing. I showed him my winter training book, where I recorded all my workouts. He slowly went through it and started smiling. He told me I clearly had been bitten by the bug. While I had not thought about it, I guess I had been bitten pretty hard. Otherwise why was I going through all this?

Despite my weak showings, I liked the races and the competition. I was not a challenge to anyone other than beginning rowers. I was the guy who paid the entry fees to feed someone else's glory. For some reason the fifty-year-old group was extremely competitive, and in many races the group's times were better than those of the forty-year–olds. I can conjecture why this was, but it does not matter. I knew that to get better I had to be in much better shape, which would take time. I also had to put time in on the water. I had to learn to be one of those rowers who doesn't look like he's rowing hard but whose boat is flying.

So I trained, with Ed and in my single. I erged and lifted and rowed. It had been almost a year since I started this crazy sport. I was able to row more than 2000 meters without dying. I was starting to understand the stroke. I was beginning to see faults and strengths in other's rowing. I was working hard. I still did not like all the spandex. But I had one last race, Head of the Schuylkill in Philadelphia.

On the day of the race, Ed and I drove down to Philadelphia mid-morning as we had an early afternoon race. Meredith was coming later with some of her best rowing friends. Her race was in the late afternoon. When we got to the race, we took our stuff to the trailer and did the pre-race relaxation and organization. We watched a few of the races as the rowers went by. Is it just me, or do other rowers find watching rowing to be a bit boring? I like the rowing, but the watching is not that interesting. For head races there is no way to tell if a boat is ahead or behind the rest of field. You can tell if they are doing better than the boats immediately before or after them by the cushion between the boats. But that is about it. Not a very dynamic spectator sport. Bowling has more action. At least the ball crashes into the pins that end up flying all over. How was this sport of rowing so popular in the late 1800s? Was life that boring then?

Soon enough it was time for Ed and me. As we took the boat down to the water, I went through my mental checklist. Row hard for about twenty minutes at a 28-stroke rate. That was about all I had in my list. Not a lot going on up there. I had no clue whom the good rowers were. I had no clue where we were starting relative to the faster boats. I had no clue if the boats behind us were good, bad or indifferent boats. I had not practiced the 5 Ps. I am a CATIP rower. We got into the boat and pushed off for the start.

The Schuylkill is a nice venue. It is scenic with many boat clubs up and down the river. I did not understand why more masters were not at this race. It was the weekend after the Head of the Charles, and the race had been plagued by bad weather in the last few years. But there are tons of rowers in the Philly area with lots of boathouses are all over the Philly area. Where was everyone? Then it struck me. This is good for me. Light competition may give me a chance to finish better. Perhaps I was facing another Mystic. As we rowed to the start, my optimism rose.

Soon enough, our boat was called. We accelerated toward the start to break the timer. I settled to a 28-stroke rate and began the long row down the river. The boat was feeling good. I picked up the power a bit but kept the stroke rate. About a quarter through the race, the boat just behind us was making a noticeable move to catch up to us. It was not as obvious as at the Housatonic, but they were creeping up on us. Despite their obvious speed advantage, I was not going to crack the 28-stroke rate. I was not going to fall to 26 and try to row with more power. I kept at 28, and I kept the power in an attempt to keep them off our stern. Slowly with every stroke, they were gaining on us. We persevered as best we could. At about the two-thirds mark of the race they were able to get by us. We had put up a good fight but had lost.

Shortly after they had passed us, the boat began to feel heavier and heavier. I was extremely tired. I was having trouble keeping up the power. After a few more minutes I just could not keep up the power any longer and had to bring down the oar pressure a couple of notches. I had committed a grievous error: fly and die. I went out too fast and hard and did not have enough for the rest of the race. In running terms I had been the rabbit. Sadly, a slow rabbit that was easy to catch and pass. But I could not quit; as the rabbit does in a long running race. I had to finish the race.

Ed said nothing. A less gentlemanly partner might have started yelling. A more normal human might have bitched to the coaches about the shape I was in. A normal human would be telling me that I sucked and to get in better shape. But Ed just kept plugging along. He is a diesel engine of a rower.

As we got closer to the finish, Ed yelled for another 50 strokes. If I had the ability to talk then, I would have asked for him to verify. But I was beat and knew I had to give him more now that we were close. I prayed that we only had 50 strokes and not some number well north of that. I picked up the power and the stroke rate to 30. During this 50 strokes we passed a slower boat. Since passing a boat was a first for us, my adrenaline kicked in and carried me to the finish.

We finally heard the finish horn about 48 strokes later. I was too beat to say anything to Ed. I was too tired to say, I thought you said 50 not 48. The smart ass in me had been ground to nothing due to lack of the oxygen to my brain. My lungs felt bad and my legs felt bad. I began to wonder if any rower had suffered cardiac arrest at the end of a race. I slowly regained enough bodily function to help Ed row us back to the dock. We pulled the boat out of the water and were immediately met by the coaches. What had happened? Why did you slow down? What happened after that boat passed you?

I looked at one of the coaches and said, "Sorry. I guess I suck," which pretty much sums up my first year of racing. We finished next-to-last in this race. But we were only a little over two minutes off the winning pace. *Only*. You can always find a ray of sunshine in your performance if you look at the times of other boats. For example, as bad as we stunk up the race, we were still ahead of many the women's quads. We were a double and they were a quad. But a refrain from an old coach keeps coming back to me when I do this type of analysis: you can excuse bad performance any way you want, but it is still bad performance. In the immortal words of Rickie Bobby, "If you are not first, you're last."

19

A Year of Rowing

My rowing career had now lasted a little more than a year. I had sweat like I was a teenager. I had worked at this sport as I had not worked at any sport in many, many years. I was in the kind of shape that most would be extremely happy about. But it was still not good enough for the sport of my choice.

I had become a bit obsessive about rowing. I wrote down workouts. I compared splits. I pushed harder if my workout times were off. I could tell you how much low-cardio I had done in a week, how much threshold, and how much work I had done over threshold. I wore a heart-rate monitor and would religiously go through it at the end of the workout to verify my heart-rate levels. I was doing lactic acid tests every few months to track and adjust my progress to the fitness levels I needed. My son was right: I had been bitten.

Despite the obsessive rituals I was following, I had stunk in just about every race. I had left my bad rowing stank up and down the eastern seaboard. I was no threat to anyone in a race. If I stopped the sport today, there would be no trail of my rowing existence. Google my name and no race results would come up. I am a nonexistent rower.

Though my rowing stunk like week-old fish, I had learned to enjoy the sport. Being out on the water was nice. No matter how hard you worked, the osprey diving on a bait fish or a bunker jumping in the water or dodging the boat traffic seemed to make the day a little bit more alive. I met people of all stripes—the committed to rowing and the sort of committed, liberal save-the-earthers, and Ross Perot twins. But one thing that is common to these people is their love for a sport. I am still amazed at how many adults begin the sport after their children started rowing in high school. How could watching your children go through the exercise pain this sport requires inspire an adult to begin rowing? I still do not get it, but a number of rowers at our club started after watching their children row in high school.

I have read most of the books about rowing. Some were training and self-help books; others described the mystical beauty of the sport. I don't think I have transcended into the mystical part of rowing. When I read or hear others talk about the sport's beauty, I do not get shivers. Do you remember the first time you saw an NFL running back in super slow motion? You see the eyes, you see the cut and acceleration for the opening, and you see the bone-crushing tackle. If you do the same slow motion for rowing, you merely see a person rowing. You might see some heavy breathing and maybe a small facial twitch from the aerobic pain. But that is it. No drama there. It just seems like a lot of hard work.

But I like the camaraderie of the club. And I like the competition. Sometimes I wonder if I ever win a race, will I meet the magic man and transcend myself? I wonder if when you are in the kind of shape needed for elite competition, the endorphin levels in your blood cause you to feel high. Maybe this transcendental endorphin high is just a bong replacement. Who knows? For now, I shut up and row. Okay—I cannot always keep my mouth closed.

Shortly after the end of the racing season, our coaches asked us to do a 2000-meter erg test. At our club, these tests are about as welcome as the plague. If the weather is good for rowing, it seems like the club is loaded with rowers. But if it is the day of a 2K test, many club members have previous commitments. Hmmmmm.

These races are painful. They take an all-out effort for seven or eight minutes. They do not make you feel good. And as you age it gets increasingly hard to match the times of your earlier years. So it is not surprising that something gets in the way of showing up at the club on that day. Given that Marlene wanted a 2K race time on which to base my next winter's training, I felt stuck. So I cancelled my "previous commitment" and showed up that day. I had never done a 2K and was not especially excited about the pain I was to go through.

I got to the club and did a pre-race warm-up. I watched some of the other rowers doing their race. It was more of a delaying tactic than a true interest in my fellow rowers. Nonetheless, I yelled excitedly when someone was pulling a good race on the erg. About that time one of the coaches pointed to an erg and told me to sit down. Yikes! I went to the erg while the coach set up the timer for the race.

Since I had never done a 2K, I was unsure how hard to pull on the erg. I knew that last winter, a two-minute split for 500 meters seemed hard. But I thought I was in better shape now. So as I had done for most of my short rowing career, I decided go out hard and see how it went. I was hoping that I did not pull a Schuylkill where I did the "fly and die." I got myself mentally ready and started hard.

For the first 500 meters I went as hard as I thought made sense. It was hard but doable so I stayed close to that same split for the next 500 meters. I was about done with my third 500-meter piece when the coach came over and put a post it note on my erg timer with the number 7:40 on it. Despite my heavy breathing I knew that he wanted me to pull that time for the entire 2K race. I went into overdrive for the last 500 meters. I did not think I could get to that time unless I pulled a much lower split. The coach was talking me through it, trying to encourage me and yelling numbers that he wanted me to hit. What he said was not being processed by my brain. It was the tone of his voice that told me he wanted me to go faster. So faster I went.

I was getting tired and was now counting strokes to try and keep my mind off the effort I was putting in. At the end of the 2K the coach patted me on the back and pointed to my timer. I had pulled a 7:39. I had beaten his goal. I wanted to see what my splits were for the entire race so I checked the memory on the timer. The splits were:

500m	1:56
1000m	1:57
1500m	1:56
2000m	1:48

This is not a classic race-split scenario. When a coach looks at this, the coach would probably tell the athlete that the early splits should have been lower. The coach would say that I could have probably taken five to ten seconds off my total time with a better race strategy.

At the time I really didn't care. I had done a 2K at a pace that I would not have been capable of six months before. Even though no one would call me fast by rowing standards, I was no longer a cardio disaster- a back-bencher, but not a disaster. I felt good about my progress.

I was a slow racer with a less-than-successful first racing season. But all that work had had results that were undeniable. My blood pressure was down. My good cholesterol was better while the bad stuff was down. I wish I could say I had adopted the Craftsbury diet, but it would be a lie. I still like my cured meats. Steak still ranks up there as one of my favorite meals. I have not gotten into the whole organic, healthy living thing. I am not sure I really believe all the hype. Quaker Oats granola tastes better than the organic crud. I still do not get misty talking about whole grains or organic lettuce. But I am eating better. More fruit and vegetables, less red meat and definitely more water. I have not yet cracked the diet soda habit. But I have cracked the diet cola with breakfast habit. Michelle Guerette, who won a silver medal in women's singles rowing at the 2008 Olympics in Beijing, supposedly eats Pop Tarts before a race. Clearly, then, my dining habits are not the issue with my performance on the water.

I still hate those damn shorts, and I hate the tight shirts that seem to amplify my Michelin man appearance. The shirts the men wear at regattas are called tanks. They are like tight basketball shirts from my youth. Not a pretty sight for my competitors when they see me in one of these with my club colors emblazoned on it. Maybe one day someone will look over and think I am an imposing rower instead of the slouchy troll they see now. Maybe I will shave my head and eyebrows and get a rowing tattoo on my calf that is visible to the other rowers at the start of races. If I cannot beat them with my skills, I will beat them with my scary appearance.

After this year of rowing I could not help wondering whether, given the knowledge I have now, I would advise someone to take this journey. I think so, but why would anyone listen to me? I am a crap rower. I envy those that can do it well. I envy rowers who can row a 36 SPM and make it look like they are doing 24. My 36 still looks like a splash fest.

I am getting closer on the fitness. After the 2k test, we went for lactic acid testing, and my threshold was a little over 200 watts. Still not in the 230's but getting closer. Another round of winter training, and maybe I will be even closer. Guenter had been right—two years to get in shape and probably four to be competitive.

I get asked occasionally if all this exercise has helped me with my focus, attention span, or other parts of my life (which is guy code for sex). I sleep a bit better, and I have a bit more energy. I also have seen the health benefits. I have not had any karmic experiences nor do I expect to. I still get pissed-off at work and at home at times. But there seems to be less stress. Somehow getting on an erg or out on the water and sweating large amounts of salty water seems to take the starch out of most problems.

I have lost weight. But when I look at pictures of me, I still see a bulky boy. Age is a bit like that. I have read that your waistline slowly expands as you get older no matter what kind of shape you are in. But when I line up at a race and see all these fifty-five-year-old men and women with little body fat, I feel a bit like a porker. But the good news is that it makes me want to work harder. I sort of figure if they can do it, so can I. I am not sure I will get there, but I realize that's not important. It is only important that I make an effort. I know that competing with men my age who were on the national team or Olympic team or rowed in college is a huge hurdle. I will whack away and try to get better technically and aerobically.

I still have trouble starting workouts. I will delay by any means necessary. But once I push away from the dock, I tend to be fairly committed. I want to be left alone during a workout. You will not get me into too many conversations while working out, on or off the water. I always figure there is more work than I have the time or the commitment to do. So get the workout done. Do what you need to do and leave it on the water.

Many will say that my children must be proud of me for losing weight and getting back into shape. I hope so, but to them Dad is Dad. The oldest likes to hear about what we are doing in our workouts and what medals Meredith has won. The younger boys do not really notice much. They tell me I am a fat old thing and are more embarrassed about the spandex than I am. Kids are kids and like many things we do as adults, our children only notice later in life. As a parent, I hope that they will find their own athletic niche that they can take into the later years of their life and stay in better shape than their old man has done.

I am still surprised by how committed I am to this sport. This is the first aerobic-based sport I have ever enjoyed. I hate running distances. I like biking but not enough to be committed to being competitive. Swimming is okay in small doses. But rowing has gotten under my skin. Most boomer Southerners grew up knowing nothing about rowing. Like hockey, you only knew it existed. The first memory I have of any contact with rowing was when a guy from my high school graduated and went to Brown University and became part of the rowing team there. But his parents were British. We figured it was a Brit thing.

Due to Title IX, the South is experiencing some of the fastest growth in rowing. Alabama, Clemson, U. of South Carolina, Duke, Oklahoma and U. of North Carolina have women's rowing teams. The beautiful river running through the center of Austin, Texas, is the home of the University of Texas rowing team as well as a number of private clubs. There are nice sprint racing venues in Oakridge, Tennessee, and head races are held in Chattanooga and Oklahoma City. So a sport that has traditionally been defined as a Northeast and West Coast sport is migrating. There are an increasing number of private boathouses all throughout the South where masters rowers congregate.

I have been struck by how tightly knit rowing is. I have met Olympic rowers, Olympic coaches, and national team rowers from the U.S. and other countries. I have been trained by folks with unbelievable resumes, and I am nothing in the sport. A coach at our club can give you the resume of practically every top rower over the last twenty years. Meredith competed at the Crash Bs, the world indoor rowing championship, in the winter of 2008. Amazingly, her coach gave her the rundown on the competition off the top of her head. I cannot think of another sport that is this tightly knit.

I spent the better part of a year working hard, becoming committed, and learning to love a sport. It was time again for winter training. No one looks forward to winter training. A lot of erg work and weight lifting is not as much fun as being on the water. But if the next year produces a similar amount of fitness progress, maybe I will be competitive. If I ever win a race, maybe I will ditch Meredith's advice and go commando under my rowing shorts. Maybe.

7700201R0

Made in the USA
Lexington, KY
09 December 2010